THIS IS HOW WE DO IT

Student Success in Higher Education & Beyond

Ajay Khanna

ISBN 979-8-89067-706-8

Aaradhya, as you prepare to embark on this exciting journey into higher education, we want to take a moment to express how incredibly proud we are of the amazing person you've become. This is a significant milestone in your life, and we have no doubt that you are well-prepared to face the challenges and adventures that await you.

Remember, this phase of your life is not just about gaining knowledge and earning a degree; it's an opportunity to explore, grow, and discover who you truly are. Embrace each moment, savour every experience, and never be afraid to step out of your comfort zone.

While you'll encounter obstacles and setbacks along the way, please know that we have complete faith in your ability to overcome them. You've always shown resilience, determination, and a thirst for learning, qualities that will serve you well in this new chapter.

Stay true to yourself, stay focused on your goals, and always seek to expand your horizons. Your journey into higher education is a stepping stone towards a bright future, and we can't wait to see the incredible things you'll achieve.

Always remember that we're here for you, cheering you on every step of the way. Don't hesitate to reach out whenever you need advice, support, or simply a friendly chat.

Mom & Dad

CONTENTS

Introduction

Imagine having a trusted companion in your life, someone with all the answers to your burning questions about college and what lies beyond. Having a confidant who offers judgement-free guidance, where no question is too trivial, and you can inquire with unwavering confidence. Think about those lingering questions you've always wanted to ask but hesitated. Well, here's your moment—a dynamic, interactive Guide, a Mentor by your side, ready to assist you through every step of your higher education journey and beyond. Welcome to the world of *This is How We Do It*.

This Is How We Do It: Student Success in Higher Education and Beyond holds immense importance, as it seeks to revolutionise the concept of student success in the present landscape. This book is an earnest endeavour to help students discover their true potential, identify opportunities, and fearlessly thrive in their academic and professional pursuits.

Based on my extensive experience of working with countless students in higher education, *This Is How We Do It* reflects my strong belief that every student holds exceptional talents and untapped potential. As a passionate advocate for students, I have witnessed the determination that burns within them to carve a meaningful space for themselves. However, many face uncertainties and challenges, unsure of where to begin their journey. Some may hesitate to seek guidance, while others lack access to essential resources.

Through writing this book, my primary mission is to distil the complexities of higher education and offer actionable solutions to empower thousands of individuals in achieving success through their unique paths. *This Is How We Do It* encompasses a wealth of strategies for excelling in higher education and beyond, all derived from my practical insights and first-hand experiences as a learning & development leader in the corporate sector, director of student success at a university level, and now as a career coach and author.

Each page of this guide is meticulously crafted to help students, providing them with invaluable tips and tools for navigating the academic landscape and preparing for the ever-evolving professional world. I aim to bridge the gap between aspirations and accomplishments, ensuring that students are equipped with the knowledge and skills required to thrive.

This book addresses unasked questions, providing a safe space for students to learn from a neutral perspective and make informed decisions. As a reliable coach, it offers clarity on various aspects of higher education and beyond.

From this comprehensive book, students will learn essential skills to:

1. Navigate the higher education landscape confidently, making informed choices for a successful career path.

2. Understand the dynamics of the job world, preparing effectively for various opportunities.

3. Develop strategies to manage relationships effectively, enhancing personal and professional growth.

So, are you ready to take control of your student success journey? It all starts here, and I'm thrilled to be your guide. Let's dive in and make your educational and professional dreams a reality!

CHAPTER 1

RETHINKING STUDENT SUCCESS: BEYOND GRADES

Let's start with the most important question — What is student success in higher education? Is it just about grades and academic achievements? I've encountered this question many times. In this chapter, let's redefine student success and explore a more holistic approach. Let's challenge the existing societal definition and explore a broader perspective that goes beyond the traditional markers of success. I strongly believe that success in higher education and beyond is not just about academics but also personal growth, social responsibility, and overall well-being.

Academic excellence is definitely important but it is just one piece of the puzzle. Let's rethink the idea that success can be measured by a number or a letter on a transcript. What about qualities like compassion, leadership, and a sense of purpose? Don't they hold immense value in shaping individuals into responsible citizens and empathetic human beings?

At its core, student success should be viewed as a multidimensional concept that encompasses intellectual growth, personal development, social responsibility, and emotional well-being. It is an ongoing journey of self-discovery, exploration, and growth that extends beyond the confines of the classroom. Here's my perspective on what true student success entails:

PERSONAL GROWTH AND SELF-AWARENESS

True success is an ongoing journey of self-reflection and personal growth. It involves exploring passions, values, and strengths, and aligning them with academic pursuits.

Self-reflection allows you to delve into your thoughts and aspirations, gaining clarity and insight. It uncovers genuine interests and areas of excellence, helping you make informed decisions about your academic and career path.

Aligning academic pursuits with passions and values creates a sense of purpose, infusing education with meaning. It motivates you to invest in subjects and activities that resonate with your desires, leading to a deeper sense of engagement and commitment.

Developing self-awareness aids in setting meaningful goals, and identifying strengths and areas for improvement. This enables you to set realistic targets, design a personalised roadmap for growth, and achieve success.

SOCIAL RESPONSIBILITY AND COMMUNITY ENGAGEMENT

True student success goes beyond personal growth and achievements. It's about making a positive impact on others and the world.

It's not just about excelling academically or landing a dream job; it's about using our abilities to benefit others. This broader perspective empowers us to create a meaningful impact beyond ourselves.

Community service is vital for social responsibility. Volunteering helps marginalised communities and vulnerable populations, contributing to the betterment of society. Experiences like food drives or tutoring underprivileged students develop empathy and compassion.

Advocating for causes that matter to us raises awareness about social issues and promotes equity and inclusivity. Our involvement can bring about meaningful change in areas like gender equality, environmental sustainability, and human rights.

EMOTIONAL INTELLIGENCE AND WELL-BEING

Another essential aspect of student success is emotional well-being. Understanding and managing emotions and relationships are vital for personal growth alongside career goals.

Building resilience is crucial to bounce back from challenges. Academic journeys involve tough coursework and high expectations. Resilience enables positivity and adaptability, turning setbacks into opportunities for growth.

Seeking support when needed is a sign of strength. Reach out for help with academic, personal, or emotional challenges. Early assistance prevents issues from escalating, and universities provide ample support for students. Don't hesitate to ask for help or offer it to others in need.

LEADERSHIP AND COLLABORATION

Leadership is a vital aspect of success, extending beyond formal titles or positions. It is a mindset that involves taking initiative, embracing responsibility, and making a positive impact in various aspects of life. Developing leadership skills during your higher education days prepares you to navigate the complexities of the professional world and contribute meaningfully to society.

- Effective communication is at the core of leadership. It involves the ability to articulate ideas clearly, listen actively, and engage in constructive dialogue. Strong communication skills enable students to collaborate effectively, express their thoughts and perspectives, and inspire others to take action.

- Teamwork is another crucial aspect of leadership. Collaborating with others, valuing diverse perspectives, and leveraging the strengths of each team member are essential for achieving common goals.

- Problem-solving is a key leadership skill that involves analysing complex situations, identifying innovative solutions, and taking decisive action. Students who develop strong problem-solving skills can approach challenges with a growth mindset, view obstacles as opportunities for learning, and make informed decisions.

- Inclusivity and embracing diversity are integral components of modern leadership. Successful leaders create an environment where individuals from diverse backgrounds feel valued, respected, and included.

Purpose and Fulfilment

True success comes from understanding your driving forces, and passions, and aligning academic and career goals with your values. Discovering your purpose requires self-reflection and exploration. Reflect on what matters most to you and what you wish to contribute to the world. Uncover your passions and define your purpose.

Align your goals with your purpose by seeking opportunities that resonate with your values. Choose courses and activities that allow you to explore interests and make meaningful contributions.

Nurture purpose by engaging with your studies and embracing a growth mindset. Love learning and seek experiences that expand your horizons, leading to academic success and personal growth.

Factors Influencing Student Success in Higher Education

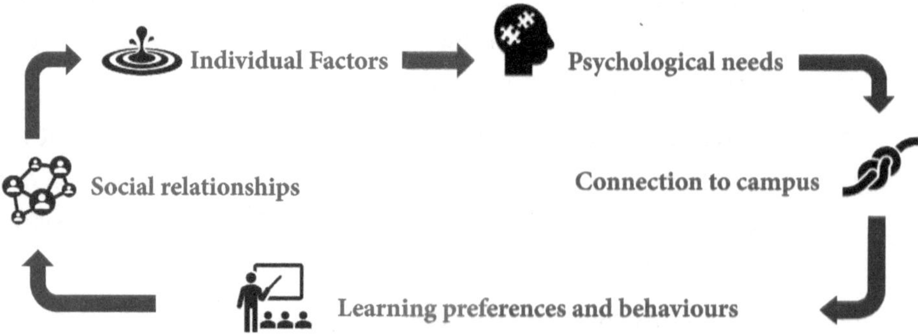

Source – Front. Educ., 29 March 2022 Educational Psychology

Factors influencing student success in higher education can be categorised into the below five categories. Let's understand each of these factors:

1. **Individual Factors:** Factors like prior academic preparedness, motivation & self-discipline, learning abilities or disabilities and financial resources are characteristics and attributes specific to each student and can impact their academic performance and overall success.

2. **Psychological Needs:** Psychological well-being plays a crucial role in academic success. The ability to manage emotions, cope with stress, and maintain a positive outlook can impact a student's focus, motivation, and overall academic performance. Having clear and meaningful academic goals can provide direction and purpose, enhancing students' commitment to their studies.

3. **Connection to Campus:** Feeling a sense of belonging to the academic institution is vital for student success. Factors like campus culture, faculty support and co-curricular activities can significantly contribute to a strong campus connection

4. **Social Relationships:** Interpersonal connections with peers, mentors, and support networks are essential for student success. Positive and supportive friendships with fellow students can contribute to a positive college experience and provide a network for academic collaboration and assistance. Having access to mentors or academic advisers who offer guidance and support can help students navigate challenges and make informed decisions about their academic journey.

5. **Learning Preferences and Behaviours:** Students have diverse learning styles and behaviours that influence their academic achievements. Understanding and aligning with one's preferred learning style, whether visual, auditory, or kinesthetics, can enhance information retention and comprehension.

INTEGRATED MODEL OF STUDENT SUCCESS

The Student Success Model presented below is the result of my extensive experience working closely with over 20,000 students pursuing higher education. Through my interactions with these students, from diverse backgrounds and academic disciplines, I have identified key components that contribute to their overall success and fulfilment.

The model is designed to provide a comprehensive framework that captures the multifaceted nature of student success. It acknowledges that success is not solely defined by grades or academic accomplishments but also by personal development, social responsibility, and the ability to find purpose and fulfilment in one's pursuits.

This model reflects the common patterns and themes observed across various educational contexts. It serves as a guide to help students navigate their educational journey and make informed choices that contribute to their holistic growth and success.

By considering the different dimensions outlined in this model and striving for a balanced approach, students can enhance their overall well-being, build strong foundations for their careers, and make meaningful contributions to society.

Let's explore these points briefly to understand the meaning of each component.

- **Academic Excellence (30%):** This aspect represents the mastery of academic subjects, achieving high grades, and demonstrating a strong understanding of the curriculum. It includes performing well in exams, assignments, and projects.

- **Personal Growth (20%):** Personal growth encompasses the development of essential life skills, self-awareness, emotional intelligence, and resilience. It includes aspects such as self-reflection, personal values, and the ability to handle challenges and setbacks effectively.

- **Leadership and Communication Skills (15%):** This aspect focuses on developing leadership qualities, effective communication skills, and the ability to work well in teams. It includes activities like participating in group projects, taking leadership roles in student organisations, and demonstrating strong interpersonal skills.

- **Social Engagement and Community Service (15%):** This component emphasises the importance of actively participating in community service, volunteering, and engaging in social initiatives. It includes activities that contribute to the welfare of society and promote a sense of social responsibility.

- **Professional Readiness (10%):** Professional readiness refers to the acquisition of skills, knowledge, and experiences that prepare students for their future careers. It includes internships, job-related experiences, networking, and career development activities.

- **Well-being and Work-Life Balance (10%):** This aspect recognises the significance of maintaining physical and mental well-being and achieving a healthy work-life balance. It includes practising self-care, managing stress effectively, and nurturing personal interests and hobbies.

CHAPTER 2

UNDERSTANDING THE HIGHER EDUCATION LANDSCAPE

Higher education serves as a catalyst that propels individuals towards their dreams, equipping them with the tools to shape a brighter future. As the world rapidly evolves, so does the landscape of higher education, transforming into a dynamic realm of boundless possibilities. This chapter delves into the evolving landscape in India and the remarkable emergence of the country as a global leader in education.

India's higher education landscape presents a blend of progress and challenges. It boasts an extensive scope with a staggering number of institutions. According to the latest All India Survey of Higher Education Report (AISHE 2020–21), the total number of universities / university-like institutions registered is 1,113, Colleges 43,796 and standalone institutions 11,296 making it one of the largest higher education sectors globally. Enrolment in higher education has increased to 4.14 crore, crossing the 4 crore mark for the first time; an increase of 7.5% from 2019-20 and 21% from 2014-15. Female enrolment reached the 2 crore mark, an increase of 13 lakhs from 2019-20.

*Ref.- AISHE 2020–21

The growth of institutions has been remarkable, expanding by over 400% since 2001. Notably, a significant portion of this growth has occurred in the private education sector, as highlighted in the Brookings Institution's comprehensive 2019 report titled "Reviving Higher Education in India". This trend continued throughout 2019-20, as indicated by the 2019-20 AISHE report.

India, with its rich cultural heritage and diverse demographic, has witnessed a paradigm shift in the higher education sector. In recent years, the country has experienced a remarkable surge in the establishment of private universities, driven by provisions under the law. This transformative wave has shattered conventional notions, amplifying the accessibility and quality of education, and paving the way for students to explore a plethora of educational pathways.

When compared to the global higher education industry, India's growth stands out. While established education systems in countries like the United States and the United Kingdom have long been renowned, India has rapidly caught up, propelling itself as a leading force in education. The country's dedication to academic excellence and continuous improvement has propelled it onto the global stage, challenging traditional academic powerhouses. Every one of India's 28 states and five of the eight union territories (Chandigarh, Delhi, Jammu and Kashmir, Ladakh, and Puducherry) is home to universities. Among these states, Rajashthan now stands out with the highest number of universities, boasting a total of 92. Gujarat leads in private universities, with an impressive count of 60, far surpassing other states in this regard.

THE NATIONAL EDUCATION POLICY AND ITS IMPACT ON STUDENT DEVELOPMENT

The National Education Policy (NEP) of India, which was approved in 2020, aims to transform the country's education system and plays a crucial role in strengthening India's position globally. Built on the foundational pillars of Access, Equity, Quality, Affordability and Accountability, this policy is aligned with the 2030 Agenda for Sustainable Development and aims to transform India into a vibrant knowledge society and global knowledge superpower by making both school and college education more holistic, flexible, multidisciplinary, suited to 21st century needs and aimed at bringing out the unique capabilities of each student. Students in higher education are set to benefit significantly from the National Education Policy (NEP) in various ways:

Flexible learning options and multidisciplinary approaches.	Skill development for enhanced employability.	Opportunities for research and innovation.	Global exposure through collaborations.

Emphasis on critical thinking and problem-solving.	Integration of technology for improved learning.	Holistic development and recognition of diverse talents

- **Flexibility and Multidisciplinary Learning:** Students will have the opportunity to choose from a wide range of subjects and create their own unique learning pathways. This enables them to explore diverse fields of interest and develop a holistic understanding of various subjects, fostering creativity and adaptability.

- **Skill Development and Employability:** Students will receive training in relevant skills, making them more employable and prepared to meet the evolving needs of the job market. This focus on practical skills ensures that graduates are job-ready and capable of contributing effectively to the workforce.

- **Research and Innovation Opportunities:** With an increased emphasis on research and innovation, students in higher education will have more opportunities to engage in cutting-edge research projects.

- **Global Exposure:** This provides students with opportunities for international exchanges, joint research programmes, and exposure to diverse cultures and perspectives. Such global exposure enhances their understanding of global issues and prepares them to become global citizens.

- **Focus on Critical Thinking and Problem-Solving:** By encouraging deeper understanding and application of knowledge, students will be better equipped to address complex real-world challenges and make informed decisions.

- **Integration of Technology:** By integrating technology into the learning process, students will have access to innovative teaching methods, online resources, and digital learning platforms, enhancing their learning experience and accessibility to quality education.

- **Holistic Development:** The NEP aims to nurture the overall development of students, including their physical, emotional, and mental well-being. By providing a holistic and nurturing environment, students can flourish academically and personally, leading to overall growth and a balanced approach to life.

- **Recognition of Non-Traditional Skills:** This ensures that students with different interests, such as sports, arts, or vocational skills, are given equal opportunities to excel and pursue their passions alongside their academic pursuits.

THE RISE OF INDIA AS A GLOBAL LEADER IN EDUCATION

India's ascent as a global leader in education is not merely a matter of numbers, but also the calibre of institutions and the quality of education they provide. Esteemed Indian universities, such as the Indian Institutes of Technology (IITs), Indian Institutes of Management (IIMs), and Jawaharlal Nehru University (JNU), and many private universities have garnered international recognition for their academic prowess and research contributions. These institutions consistently rank among the top in global assessments and rankings, alongside renowned universities in the Western world.

As per London-based global higher education analyst, Quacquarelli Symonds's (QS) recently published the QS World University Rankings 2023, featuring over 1400 universities worldwide, 41 Indian universities have made the list, an increase from 35 last year. Among them, 12 institutions have improved their positions, 12 maintain their ranks, and 10 have slipped. Additionally, seven new Indian institutions made their debut on the list.

The Indian Institute of Science (IISc) Bangalore, the top-ranked Indian university, has made a significant leap of 31 places from 2022, now ranked at 155th position. Other prominent Indian universities include IIT Bombay (=172), IIT Delhi (=174), IIT Madras (250), and IIT Kanpur (=264). This is another compelling evidence of how well Indian universities are performing on the global stage.

The global impact of Indian higher education is also evident through collaborations with esteemed international universities. These partnerships foster cross-cultural exchanges, enabling students and faculty to engage in collaborative research, knowledge sharing, and academic mobility. Indian institutions actively participate in global academic networks and initiatives, contributing to the advancement of knowledge on an international scale.

Furthermore, the rise of Massive Open Online Courses (MOOCs) and digital learning platforms has expanded the reach and influence of Indian higher education globally. These initiatives allow learners across the world to access Indian educational resources and expertise, breaking down geographical barriers and democratising education.

COMPARISON WITH GLOBAL COUNTERPARTS

When compared to its global counterparts, the Indian higher education industry offers unique strengths and opportunities. While Western universities have long been regarded as prestigious, India's educational landscape presents distinctive advantages, particularly in terms of affordability and diversity. India offers a range of programmes at a significantly lower cost compared to many Western countries, making quality education more accessible to a larger population. This affordability, coupled with a rich cultural milieu, attracts students from diverse backgrounds and fosters a vibrant and inclusive learning environment.

Moreover, India's demographic dividend—a large, youthful population—provides a unique advantage. With a significant percentage of its population comprising young individuals, India has a vast talent pool that contributes to the vitality and innovation within its higher education institutions. This demographic advantage positions India as a global leader, as it can produce a skilled workforce equipped to address emerging challenges and drive economic growth.

INFRASTRUCTURE COMPARISON OF INDIAN HIGHER EDUCATION WITH WORLD UNIVERSITIES

The infrastructure of higher education institutions plays a vital role in providing a conducive learning environment and facilitating research and innovation. While Indian higher education institutions have made significant progress in recent years, there are areas where they can further enhance their infrastructure to match the standards set by world-class universities.

In terms of physical infrastructure, Indian institutions have witnessed substantial growth in recent years. Many universities have invested in modern classrooms, well-equipped laboratories, libraries with extensive digital resources, and student support facilities. Renovation and expansion projects have transformed campuses, providing students with a vibrant and conducive environment for learning and personal growth.

To compete with global universities, Indian institutions are increasingly focusing on creating world-class research and innovation centres. These centres serve as hubs for cutting-edge research, interdisciplinary collaboration, and knowledge exchange. For example, the Indian Institute of Science (IISc) in Bangalore and the Indian

Institutes of Technology (IITs) have established research centres that are at par with global standards. These centres not only foster advanced research but also attract international collaborations and renowned faculty.

There is definitely room for further development in infrastructure to meet the growing demands of research and innovation. Investments in state-of-the-art laboratories, advanced research equipment, and technology infrastructure will empower students and faculty to conduct ground-breaking research and stay at the forefront of knowledge creation.

Private universities in India have played a significant role in driving infrastructure too, reshaping the educational landscape of the country. Fuelled by their autonomy and financial capabilities, these institutions have made impressive strides in expanding their campuses and enhancing facilities to meet the evolving needs of students.

Private universities have invested heavily in state-of-the-art infrastructure. From cutting-edge research centres and well-equipped laboratories to advanced libraries and digital classrooms, these institutions have spared no effort in ensuring that students have access to world-class resources and technology. Additionally, they have also prioritised the development of comfortable and safe residential facilities, creating vibrant campus communities that foster a conducive atmosphere for learning and personal growth.

RESEARCH IN INDIAN HIGHER EDUCATION

Research is a cornerstone of higher education institutions globally, contributing to scientific advancements, innovation, and societal progress. India has recognised the importance of research and has been making significant efforts to promote a research-oriented culture within its higher education institutions.

Indian universities, including private institutions, have been actively engaged in research across various fields. Here are some key data points and observations:

a. **Quantity of Research Publications:** Indian universities, both public and private, have been steadily increasing their research output. According to data from Scopus, an abstract and citation database, the number of research publications from Indian institutions has been consistently rising over the years. Private universities have contributed significantly to this growth by establishing world-class research centres and encouraging faculty and students to participate in research activities.

b. **Focus on STEM Fields:** Science, Technology, Engineering, and Mathematics (STEM) fields have been a major focus of research in Indian universities. Research in areas such as computer science, engineering, pharmaceuticals, biotechnology, and material sciences has seen substantial growth, with contributions from private universities as well.

c. **Patents and Intellectual Property:** Indian universities, including private institutions, have been filing patents and securing intellectual property rights for their research innovations. This indicates an increasing emphasis on commercialising research outcomes and fostering innovation-driven entrepreneurship.

d. **Collaborations and Funding:** Universities in India have been proactive in forming collaborations with national and international research institutions and industries. Such partnerships have facilitated access to funding for research projects, further encouraging innovation and cross-disciplinary research.

e. **Social Sciences and Humanities:** While STEM fields have dominated the research landscape, universities in India have also been actively promoting research in social sciences and humanities. There has been a growing interest in areas like psychology, economics, legal studies, and linguistics.

f. **International Recognition:** Research from Indian universities, both public and private, has gained increasing recognition on the global stage. Faculty members and researchers have received accolades, awards, and invitations to present their work at international conferences and forums.

The Indian government has demonstrated a strong commitment to promoting research and innovation by launching several strategic initiatives. The establishment of the Atal Innovation Mission, Start-up India, and various research funding agencies has been instrumental in creating an ecosystem that nurtures innovation, entrepreneurship, and research-oriented endeavours. These visionary initiatives have set the stage for collaborative efforts between academia and industry, fostering a seamless exchange of knowledge and expertise.

CHAPTER 3

LEVERAGING TECHNOLOGY FOR LEARNING

Technology has revolutionised various aspects of our lives, and education is no exception. With the rapid proliferation of smartphones, internet connectivity, and digital platforms, leveraging technology for learning has become an essential component of student success in higher education. In the Indian context, this technological shift is particularly significant, given the country's large youth population and the growing demand for quality education. In this chapter we will explore the important developments in technology-enhanced learning, how students are benefiting from it, and why both teachers and students in India must embrace technology for a brighter future.

IMPORTANT DEVELOPMENTS IN TECHNOLOGY-ENHANCED LEARNING

➤ **E-Learning Platforms:**

E-learning platforms in India have experienced remarkable growth, providing students with a wide range of educational opportunities and study materials. These platforms are web-based and often offer courses on various subjects, spanning from academic topics to professional skills development. Students can choose courses based on their interests and career aspirations, enabling them to pursue their passions and explore diverse fields beyond their traditional curriculum. The flexibility of these platforms allows students to learn at their own pace, making education more personalised and accommodating different learning styles.

⋏ Virtual Classrooms:

Virtual classrooms have emerged as a popular solution for students in remote areas who face geographical barriers to accessing quality education. Through virtual classrooms, students can participate in live lectures, discussions, and interactive sessions conducted by experienced educators from across the world. This technology has revolutionised the concept of distance learning, offering students in remote regions the same learning opportunities as those in urban centres.

⋏ Mobile Applications:

Mobile applications have revolutionised the accessibility of education, as they can be easily accessed on smartphones and tablets. These apps offer a wide range of innovative tools to enhance the learning experience. Flashcards and quizzes, for example, aid in quick and effective revision, while collaborative study groups enable students to connect with their peers for group discussions and shared learning experiences. The convenience of learning on-the-go has proven particularly beneficial for students with busy schedules, allowing them to utilise fragmented pockets of time for productive learning.

⋏ Open Educational Resources (OER):

Open Educational Resources (OER) initiatives, exemplified by the National Digital Library of India, have played a pivotal role in democratising education. By making a vast range of educational resources freely available online, OER has eliminated financial barriers that previously restricted access to textbooks, research papers, and multimedia content. Students can now access an extensive collection of learning materials without incurring additional costs, thereby reducing the financial burden of education. This initiative also promotes knowledge sharing and collaboration among students and educators, creating a community of learners who can access and contribute to a wealth of academic resources.

THE IMPORTANCE OF TECHNOLOGY FOR TEACHERS AND STUDENTS

⋏ **Digital Literacy:**

In today's modern workforce, digital skills have become essential across various industries. From basic computer proficiency to more advanced abilities like data analysis, coding, and utilising digital collaboration tools, digital literacy is a fundamental requirement for success in many careers. By integrating technology into their education, students gain practical experience and become familiar with digital tools that are prevalent in professional settings.

⋏ **Global Competitiveness:**

Students who possess strong digital skills are better equipped to compete on the global stage. India's growing role in the knowledge economy emphasises the importance of cultivating technologically adept individuals. As economies become more interconnected, businesses seek to tap into a global talent pool. Technologically proficient students can work remotely, collaborate with international teams, and participate in cross-border projects, giving India a competitive edge in the global job market.

⋏ **Innovation and Problem-Solving:**

Technology serves as a catalyst for fostering creativity, critical thinking, and problem-solving skills among students. By leveraging technology in their education, students gain access to vast resources, data, and information that can inspire innovative thinking. Additionally, technology enables hands-on learning experiences, simulations, and virtual experiments that encourage students to explore new ideas and solutions.

⋏ **Future-Ready Teaching:**

Incorporating technology effectively in the classroom transforms the role of educators, making them facilitators of knowledge rather than just information providers. Future-ready teaching involves leveraging technology to create dynamic and interactive learning environments that promote active student engagement. Educators must adapt their teaching methodologies to incorporate technology seamlessly into the curriculum, ensuring that it enhances learning outcomes rather than becoming a distraction.

Technology Usage in Indian Universities

According to a recent survey conducted by the Ministry of Education:

- Over 80% of Indian universities have integrated some form of technology-enabled learning into their curriculum.

- Nearly 60% of students reported improved academic performance due to the use of technology.

- E-learning platforms witnessed a 150% increase in enrolment during the last academic year.

Online Resources for Students

⋏ **National Digital Library of India (NDLI):** A vast repository of educational resources accessible to all students and researchers.

⋏ **SWAYAM:** An initiative offering free online courses from professors of reputed Indian universities.

⋏ **Coursera, Udemy, and Khan Academy:** Internationally acclaimed platforms providing a wide range of courses on various subjects.

⋏ **Google Scholar:** A valuable resource for academic research and access to scholarly articles.

HOW TO BENEFIT FROM TECHNOLOGY

⅄ **Goal Setting:** Start by setting clear learning objectives and identify how technology can help you achieve them. Choose appropriate technology resources, such as e-learning platforms or educational apps that align with your academic goals. Having a well-defined plan will keep you focused and on track throughout your educational journey.

⅄ **Time Management:** While technology provides the advantage of flexibility, it's crucial to manage your time effectively. Create a study schedule that incorporates technology-enabled learning sessions, and set aside specific times for focused studying. Be mindful of potential distractions from social media or unrelated websites, and use tools that help you stay on task during study sessions.

⅄ **Active Participation**: Embrace the interactive nature of technology in education by actively engaging in online discussions, forums, and virtual classrooms. Participate in group discussions, share your ideas, and ask questions to deepen your understanding of the subject matter. Actively involving yourself in the learning process will enhance your retention and critical thinking skills.

⅄ **Reach Out**: Don't hesitate to ask for help if you encounter challenges with technology or the learning material. Reach out to your professors for clarification or additional guidance. Collaborate with your peers through online study groups to learn from each other and collectively solve problems. Many educational platforms also offer online support teams or tutorials to assist you in navigating the technology effectively.

TECHNOLOGY-DRIVEN CAREER PATHWAYS

In addition to education, technology has played a pivotal role in generating numerous opportunities for students to prepare for and pursue career prospects.

- **Virtual Internships:**

  Technology has facilitated the rise of virtual internships, where students can gain work experience remotely, without the need to be physically present at the company's location. Virtual internships offer flexibility, allowing participants to work from anywhere, thereby opening up opportunities for individuals who may face geographical constraints.

- **Online Training Programmes:**

  Online training programmes, delivered through Learning Management Systems (LMS) or Massive Open Online Courses (MOOCs), offer a wide range of courses and certifications on various subjects. These programmes enable individuals to enhance their skills and knowledge conveniently, without the need to attend physical classes.

- **Virtual Workshops and Webinars:**

  Technology enables organisations and professionals to conduct virtual workshops and webinars, which are particularly valuable for large-scale knowledge dissemination and skill-building initiatives. These online events bring experts and industry leaders from different parts of the world together to share their knowledge and expertise with a global audience.

- In addition to education, technology has played a pivotal role in generating numerous opportunities for students to prepare for and pursue career prospects.

FLIPSIDE OF TECHNOLOGY IN EDUCATION AND HOW TO OVERCOME IT

1. DISTRACTIONS

Technology's abundance of entertainment and social media platforms can divert students' attention from their educational pursuits. The allure of non-educational content, such as social networking, videos, or gaming, can hinder productive study sessions.

To overcome distractions, students must cultivate self-discipline and set boundaries for technology usage during study time. Setting specific study hours and designating device-free zones can help maintain focus.

Distraction-Blocking Tools: Utilise technology to your advantage by installing distraction-blocking apps or browser extensions that limit access to non-educational websites during study sessions. These tools can enhance concentration and productivity.

Here are some popular distraction-blocking tools that can help users stay focused and improve productivity by limiting access to non-educational websites and applications during study or work sessions:

i. **Freedom:** Freedom is a versatile distraction-blocking app that works on various devices and platforms. It enables users to create custom blocklists of websites and apps to eliminate distractions during study or work periods.

ii. **Cold Turkey:** Cold Turkey is a powerful distraction-blocking software for Windows and macOS that can block websites, apps, and even specific programmes. It offers various scheduling options and a locked mode to prevent users from modifying settings during study sessions.

iii. **LeechBlock:** A Firefox extension that allows users to specify the websites they want to block and set time limits for accessing them. Once the allocated time is exhausted, the extension blocks access to those sites for the remainder of the day.

iv. **SelfControl:** An open-source application for macOS that allows users to block access to specific websites for a set duration. Even restarting the computer or deleting the application won't lift the block until the timer runs out.

v. **Focus@Will:** Focus@Will is a unique distraction-blocking tool that offers curated music channels scientifically designed to enhance focus and productivity. It helps users maintain concentration during study or work sessions.

vi.   **RescueTime:** While not a direct distraction blocker, RescueTime tracks users' online activity and provides insights into time spent on different websites and applications. It offers a clear picture of productivity and potential distractions, enabling users to make informed changes to their online habits.

vii. **Offtime:** Offtime is a mobile app for Android and iOS that helps users reduce distractions by blocking notifications, calls, and specific apps for a defined period. It promotes mindful use of devices during study or relaxation time.

Do not forget that the effectiveness of these tools depends on individual discipline and commitment to staying focused. Experiment with different tools to find the one that works best for you and aligns with your study or work habits.

2. DISPARITY

Not all students have equal access to technology due to financial limitations or living in underserved areas. This lack of access can create disparities in educational opportunities.

Educational institutions and policymakers should prioritise initiatives to bridge the technology gap. Providing students with access to devices and internet connectivity can level the playing field and ensure everyone has equal access to educational resources.

Collaboration between the community, government, and private organisations can lead to initiatives like subsidised devices or internet packages for students in need. This collaborative effort is essential to address the issue of technological disparities effectively.*

---

* Ajay Khanna has been recognised as a Top E-Learning Voice by LinkedIn

CHAPTER 4

CHOOSING THE RIGHT COURSE AND UNIVERSITY

Let me share an intriguing true story of a student named Shubham (name hidden) that I encountered during his second year of an engineering degree course. Shubham was an enthusiastic learner, always open to exploring new ideas. However, as time passed, it became evident that he wasn't content with the course he was pursuing. Trapped by the peer pressure of joining the same course as his friends, Shubham landed in this situation. Within a year, his confidence dwindled, and his performance suffered, leaving him feeling that he was not good enough. This tale is just one of the many instances where brilliant students find themselves in the wrong course, and I believe we can help prevent such situations and guide them towards their true calling. In this chapter, we'll explore how to find clarity and choose the right course and university that aligns with your passions and career aspirations.

FACTORS TO CONSIDER WHEN CHOOSING A COURSE

1. **Career Prospects and Market Demand:**

   While deciding on a course, it's essential to think about future career prospects. Do some research to find out what job opportunities are available within your chosen field of interest. Knowing the demand for professionals in that industry will give you a better idea of your job prospects after completing the course.

2.   **Personal Interests and Passions:**

Making your learning journey enjoyable is vital. Take a moment to think about what you love doing. By evaluating your interests and passions, you can find subjects or fields that align with your preferences. This way, you'll stay motivated and engaged throughout your studies.

3.   **Course Curriculum:**

What you learn in your course is super important. Take some time to review the course curriculum. Make sure it covers topics that match your goals and aspirations. A well-designed curriculum will give you the skills and knowledge you need for your dream career.

4.   **Skills and Strengths:**

Knowing your own skills and strengths is prime when choosing a course. Take a look at what you're good at, and see how they match with the skills required in the course. This way, you'll find a course that suits you and helps you shine.

5.   **Practical Exposure and Internship Opportunities:**

Practical experience is valuable for your learning. Look for courses that offer hands-on exposure and internships. Gaining real-world experience will make you more employable and ready to conquer the world.

Each of these factors matters, and there could be more, but it's up to you to decide what's most important for your educational journey. Here are simple metrics that I use to help my students to gain clarity in choosing the right course:

	1. Personal Interests and Passions (30%)	Evaluate your interests and passions. Identify subjects or fields that align with your preferences.
	2. Career Prospects and Market Demand (25)%	Research the job market and career opportunities. Determine the demand for professionals in the chosen field.
	3. Course Curriculum (15%)	Review the course curriculum and subjects offered. Ensure it covers topics that align with your goals.
	4. Skills & Strengths (15%)	Assess your skills and strengths. Match them with the required skills in the course.
	5. Practical Exposure and Internship Opportunities (15%)	Look for courses that offer practical exposure and internships. Gain hands-on experience to enhance employability.

Choosing the right course can significantly impact your career trajectory, leading to success and personal fulfilment. Let's look at some examples and data that highlight the importance of making informed choices:

1. **Alignment with Career Goals:**

    A well-chosen course that aligns with one's career goals can provide the necessary skills and knowledge for the chosen profession. For example, a student interested in a career in computer science would benefit from pursuing a degree in computer science or a related field, which would equip them with programming skills, problem-solving abilities, and industry-specific knowledge.

2. **Higher Employability and Job Opportunities:**

    Studies have shown that graduates who choose courses that align with their career aspirations have higher employability rates and increased job opportunities. A report by the National Association of Colleges and Employers (NACE) in the United States found that 72.5% of employers preferred to hire candidates with degrees directly related to the job position they were offering.

3.   **Job Satisfaction and Performance:**

Students who pursue courses they are passionate about are more likely to find satisfaction in their careers. This positive attitude towards their work can lead to better job performance and increased productivity. A study published in the Journal of Career Assessment found a positive correlation between job satisfaction and choosing a course that aligns with one's interests and values.

4.   **Higher Earning Potential:**

Choosing the right course can also impact a student's earning potential over their career.

5.   **Reduced Risk of Career Changes:**

When students make informed choices about their courses, they are less likely to switch careers later in life. This reduces the risk of time and money invested in pursuing a course that does not ultimately align with their long-term goals.

CRITICAL FACTORS TO CONSIDER WHEN CHOOSING A UNIVERSITY

Choosing the right university is a significant decision that will shape your higher education journey and future career. Thorough research and thoughtful consideration of these critical factors will ensure that you find a university that aligns with your aspirations and sets you on the path to success.

1.   **Accreditation and Recognition:** Opt for universities that are recognised and accredited by relevant authorities like the University Grants Commission (UGC) or the National Board of Accreditation (NBA). Accreditation ensures the quality and credibility of education.

2. **Course Offerings and Specialisations:** Look for universities that offer courses and specialisations aligned with your career goals and interests. Check the curriculum, faculty expertise, and practical exposure opportunities.

3. **Faculty Qualifications and Experience:** Research the faculty members' qualifications and expertise in their respective fields. Experienced and skilled faculty can provide valuable guidance and mentorship.

4. **Infrastructure and Facilities:** Assess the university's infrastructure, including classrooms, laboratories, libraries, and other amenities. A well-equipped campus fosters a conducive learning environment.

5. **Placements and Industry Connections:** Consider the university's placement record and industry connections. Universities with strong placement support and tie-ups with reputable companies can enhance job opportunities after graduation.

6. **Research and Innovation:** If you have an inclination towards research, look for universities that encourage and support research activities. Check for research collaborations and opportunities to engage in academic projects.

7. **Campus Culture and Diversity:** Evaluate the campus culture and diversity. A vibrant and inclusive campus environment fosters holistic development and exposure to different perspectives.

8. **Alumni Network:** An active and engaged alumni network can provide valuable insights, mentorship, and networking opportunities for your future career.

9. **Location and Accessibility:** Consider the university's location and accessibility. Proximity to industries or research centres related to your field can provide additional learning opportunities and practical exposure.

10. **Affordability and Scholarships:** Evaluate the cost of education and explore scholarship opportunities offered by the university or external organisations. Affordability is a crucial factor in making your final decision.

11. **Support Services:** Check if the university offers comprehensive support services like counselling, career guidance, and academic assistance. These services can help you navigate challenges and thrive in your studies.

Do's and Don'ts for Choosing a University/Institute

Do's

1. Do Research: Conduct thorough research on universities that offer courses aligned with your career goals and interests.

2. Do Visit the Campus: If possible, visit the campuses to get a feel of the atmosphere, infrastructure, and facilities.

3. Do Consider Placements: Look into the university's placement record and industry connections to assess future job prospects.

4. Do Seek Alumni Feedback: Reach out to alumni to gather insights about their experiences and career outcomes.

5. Do Factor Affordability: Consider the cost of education and explore available scholarship options.

Don'ts

1. Don't Rush the Decision: Take your time to make an informed choice; avoid making impulsive decisions.

2. Don't Overlook Campus Culture: Assess the campus culture and environment to ensure it aligns with your preferences.

3. Don't Disregard Location: Consider the university's location and accessibility for a comfortable learning experience.

4. Don't Disregard Reviews: Pay attention to reviews and feedback from current or former students to gauge the university's reputation.

5. Don't Choose Solely Based on Rankings: While rankings can be helpful, they should not be the sole determining factor.

Choosing the right academic course and university sets the foundation for a successful educational journey and future career. By making thoughtful decisions, you can pave the way for a fulfilling and successful path in higher education and beyond.

CHAPTER 5

SELF-PREPAREDNESS FOR SUCCESS

Meet Raj, a diligent college student who believed in the power of preparation. Before every exam, he'd start early, making comprehensive study notes and seeking help from his teachers whenever he needed clarification.

On the day of the exam, Raj felt confident and well-prepared. He could almost hear the catchy tunes of victory in the background. As he answered the questions, he felt a sense of pride in his hard work. And guess what? He aced the test! Raj's self-preparedness paid off, and he was over the moon.

Now, let's switch gears and meet Priya, a recent graduate with dreams of landing her dream job. She knew the key was to be well-prepared for interviews, so she researched the company thoroughly, rehearsed her answers to potential questions, and even practised her confident smile in the mirror.

When the day of her dream job interview arrived, Priya walked in with grace and self-assurance. As she showcased her skills and knowledge, she knew she was impressing the interviewers, just like a Bollywood superstar charms the audience. Soon after, she received the offer letter she had hoped for — an evidence of the power of self-preparedness.

Through the stories of Raj and Priya, you'll understand the importance of being prepared for every challenge that comes your way. In this chapter, we'll explore practical tips and strategies to unleash your potential and rise to greatness in your higher education and beyond.

THE IMPORTANCE OF SELF-PREPAREDNESS

As students, it's easy to overlook the immense power of self-preparedness in shaping our academic achievements and future career paths. This concept is not just about being organised or diligent; it's about cultivating a mindset that propels us towards personal and professional growth.

Self-preparedness unlocks our full potential by instilling the drive to constantly improve. It empowers us to face challenges head-on with confidence, knowing that we have put in the effort to equip ourselves with the necessary skills and knowledge. Moreover, it develops resilience, allowing us to bounce back from setbacks and learn from failures. Here are some benefits of being self-prepared:

- Self-preparedness is crucial for academic success and future career prospects.

- It boosts confidence during exams, presentations, and interviews.

- Being well-prepared fosters a sense of control and empowerment.

- It nurtures discipline and a strong work ethic.

- Self-preparedness encourages problem-solving skills and resourcefulness.

- Self-preparedness instils a sense of responsibility and accountability.

HOW TO PREPARE EFFECTIVELY

To prepare effectively, you need a solid plan and actionable strategies. Here are some key steps to get you started:

a. **Identifying Strengths and Weaknesses:** Acknowledging your areas of expertise empowers you to leverage them effectively in your academic pursuits and future career. Additionally, understanding your weaknesses allows you to proactively work on improving them, ensuring you don't face unnecessary obstacles in achieving your goals.

For example, if you excel at analytical thinking but struggle with public speaking, knowing this about yourself allows you to focus on honing your presentation skills. Embracing your strengths and addressing weaknesses will result in a well-rounded and competent individual ready to face any challenge.

b. **Goal Setting**: Begin by setting specific, measurable, achievable, relevant, and time-bound (SMART) goals for both short-term and long-term objectives. These goals will serve as your guiding light, providing clarity and direction throughout your academic journey. For example, if you aim to improve your grades in a particular subject, set a specific target grade and devise a plan to reach it. Breaking down the goal into smaller milestones will make it more manageable and motivating.

c. **Time Management:** Develop a structured daily and weekly schedule that balances academic commitments, extracurricular activities, and personal time. Allocate sufficient time for studying, attending classes, completing assignments, and preparing for exams. Tools like time-blocking and to-do lists can help you prioritise tasks and stay organised. By efficiently managing your time, you'll avoid last-minute cramming and reduce stress during busy periods.

d. **Ask for Feedback**: Use feedback as a valuable tool for growth. Actively seek feedback from professors, peers, or mentors to identify areas for improvement and build upon your strengths. Don't be afraid to ask questions or request clarification on challenging topics. Constructive feedback provides valuable insights that will help you fine-tune your skills and approach to learning.

e. **Welcome Challenges**: While it may be tempting to stick to your comfort zone, embracing challenges is essential for personal and intellectual growth. Don't shy away from difficult subjects or projects. Instead, view them as opportunities to stretch your abilities and develop resilience. New challenges will equip you with problem-solving skills that are invaluable in both academic and professional settings.

f. **Continuous Learning:** Develop a thirst for knowledge beyond the confines of the classroom. Engage in self-directed learning, read widely, and explore topics that intrigue you. Pursuing knowledge outside your curriculum will not only enrich your academic experience but also give you a competitive edge in your future career. Attend workshops, webinars, or seminars relevant to your field to stay updated on industry trends.

Let's consider an example of goal setting of a student named Rahul, who is pursuing a degree in Business Administration:

SPECIFIC GOAL   MEASURABLE   ACHIEVABLE   RELEVANT   TIME-BOUND

- **Specific Goal:** Rahul's specific goal is to secure a summer internship at a reputable marketing firm during his junior year.

- **Measurable:** Rahul's progress towards his goal can be measured by tracking his internship applications, networking events attended, and responses received from companies.

- **Achievable:** Rahul has taken relevant marketing courses, participated in marketing-related extracurricular activities, and has a strong academic record, making him a suitable candidate for marketing internships.

- **Relevant:** This goal aligns perfectly with Rahul's career aspirations to work in marketing after graduation. An internship at a reputed marketing firm will provide him with valuable industry experience and connections.

- **Time-bound:** Rahul sets a clear timeline to achieve his goal. He plans to secure the internship by the end of the second semester of his junior year to ensure he gains practical experience before entering his senior year.

Throughout the academic year, Rahul regularly tracks his internship applications and the responses received. If he receives interview invitations, he evaluates his performance in each interview and identifies areas for improvement. He continues to refine his resume and cover letter based on feedback to increase his chances of securing the internship.

By setting a SMART goal, and crafting a comprehensive action plan, Rahul is determined to secure a marketing internship that aligns with his career aspirations. Goal setting in this manner keeps him focused, motivated, and proactive in pursuing opportunities. With diligent effort and strategic planning, Rahul maximises his potential for success and positions himself for a promising career in marketing.

STARTING EARLY: THE KEY TO EMPOWERING SELF-PREPAREDNESS

The importance of starting your journey of self-preparedness early cannot be emphasised enough. Regardless of where you are in your academic journey, taking the first steps towards self-preparedness will have a significant impact on your long-term success. Here's a closer look at when you should start preparing and the benefits of doing so:

FRESHMAN YEAR: THE PERFECT STARTING POINT

As a freshman entering higher education, you are presented with a golden opportunity to lay the foundation for your academic and career success. This is an ideal time to establish strong study habits, academic routines, and time management skills. Here's what you can do during your freshman year:

a. **Establish Study Habits:** Use your first semester to experiment with different study techniques and find what works best for you. Develop a study schedule that allocates sufficient time for each subject while leaving room for extracurricular activities and personal interests.

b. **Get to Know Professors and Peers:** Building meaningful relationships with professors and fellow students can greatly enhance your academic experience. Attend office hours to clarify doubts, seek advice, and engage in discussions related to your coursework. Collaborating with peers can also foster a supportive learning environment.

c. **Guidance from Academic Advisers:** Academic advisers are valuable resources who can provide guidance on course selection, major requirements, and career pathways. Regularly consult with your academic adviser to ensure you're on track to meet your academic and career goals.

d. **Explore Extracurricular Opportunities:** Freshman year is an excellent time to explore different extracurricular activities that align with your interests and career aspirations. Join clubs, organisations, or student societies that complement your academic journey.

Continuing Years: Never Too Late to Begin

If you've already progressed beyond your freshman year, don't worry – it's never too late to embrace self-preparedness. Whether you're a sophomore, junior, or senior, there are numerous benefits to starting your journey now:

a. **Reflect on Past Experiences:** Take time to reflect on your academic journey thus far. Identify areas where you excelled and those that presented challenges. Learning from your experiences will inform your self-preparedness strategy moving forward.

b. **Make Adjustments:** Based on your reflections, make any necessary adjustments to your study habits, time management, and overall approach to learning. Set new academic and career goals that align with your current aspirations.

c. **Incorporate Self-Preparedness Strategies:** Actively integrate self-preparedness strategies into your academic routine. This could include seeking feedback from professors, building a professional network, and engaging in career-related activities.

d. **Pursue Internships and Career Opportunities:** While you may have missed some opportunities earlier on, there are still plenty of chances to pursue internships, part-time jobs, or research positions. Taking advantage of these opportunities will enrich your resume and provide valuable real-world experience.

Benefits of Early Self-Preparedness

1. **Competitive Advantage:** Starting early gives you a competitive edge in your academic and professional pursuits. As you build your skills and network, you position yourself as a desirable candidate for future internships and job opportunities.

2. **Confidence and Resilience:** Early self-preparedness instils confidence in your abilities and enhances your resilience. Facing challenges head-on from the beginning allows you to develop problem-solving skills and bounce back from setbacks more effectively.

3. **Maximising Opportunities:** By starting early, you maximise the opportunities available during your college years. You have more time to explore different career paths, gain internships, and participate in relevant projects or research.

4. **Holistic Development:** Self-preparedness is not solely about academics. By starting early, you can focus on holistic development, including emotional intelligence, soft skills, and personal well-

being. These aspects contribute to a well-rounded and successful individual.

Whether you're just beginning your higher education journey or are already well into it, the time to start your journey of self-preparedness is now. Develop a proactive mindset, set clear academic and career goals, and actively integrate self-preparedness strategies into your daily routine. So, start today, and let the journey of self-preparedness lead you to a future filled with limitless possibilities.

CHAPTER 6

CULTIVATING A GROWTH MINDSET

Throughout my years of experience, I have witnessed first-hand how developing a growth mindset can be a transformative element in the pursuit of success in higher education and beyond. Let's delve into the concept of a growth mindset and its profound influence on learning and personal development. By exploring the fundamental principles and effective strategies of a growth mindset, you, as students, can tap into your true potential, look at challenges as opportunities for growth, and foster resilience and a passion for continuous learning. With the inclusion of real-life examples and practical techniques, this chapter aims to help you to actively cultivate a growth mindset and embark on a journey of boundless growth and remarkable success.

UNDERSTANDING THE GROWTH MINDSET

The concept of a growth mindset, popularised by psychologist Carol Dweck, revolves around the belief that intelligence and abilities can be developed through dedication, effort, and effective strategies. It contrasts with a fixed mindset, where individuals believe their talents and intelligence are fixed traits. Embracing a growth mindset involves understanding that intelligence is not fixed, and through continuous learning and effort, individuals can improve their abilities and achieve greater success.

Embracing Challenges and Seeing Effort as a Path to Mastery

One of the fundamental aspects of a growth mindset is embracing challenges as opportunities for growth. Instead of shying away from difficult tasks, students with a growth mindset view challenges as a chance to learn, develop new skills, and expand their intellectual horizons. They understand that effort and perseverance are essential elements in the path to mastery.

Cultivating Resilience and Overcoming Setbacks

A growth mindset equips students with the resilience to bounce back from setbacks and failures. Rather than seeing failure as a permanent reflection of their abilities, students with a growth mindset perceive it as a stepping stone towards improvement. They understand that setbacks are an inherent part of the learning process and use them as valuable feedback for future growth.

Fostering a Love for Learning

A growth mindset nurtures a deep appreciation for learning as a lifelong journey. Students with a growth mindset approach education with curiosity, eagerness, and a thirst for knowledge. They see learning as a continuous process rather than a fixed destination. This mindset encourages students to explore new ideas, seek out diverse perspectives, and engage in self-directed learning beyond the confines of traditional classroom settings.

Developing Effective Learning Strategies

To cultivate a growth mindset, students can adopt effective learning strategies that promote continuous improvement. These strategies include setting goals, seeking feedback, utilising metacognition (thinking about one's own thinking), and employing deliberate practice techniques. By employing these strategies, students enhance their self-regulation, monitor their progress, and make adjustments to optimise their learning outcomes.

EMBRACING EFFORT AND PERSISTENCE

A growth mindset emphasises the importance of effort and persistence in achieving success. Students with a growth mindset understand that mastery and excellence require time, dedication, and hard work. They are willing to invest the necessary effort, seek out resources, and persist through challenges and setbacks to reach their goals.

NURTURING A POSITIVE LEARNING ENVIRONMENT

Educators and institutions play a crucial role in fostering a positive learning environment that promotes a growth mindset. By providing constructive feedback, recognising effort, and creating opportunities for collaborative learning and skill development, educators can empower students to embrace a growth mindset. Additionally, promoting a culture of intellectual curiosity, celebrating growth and progress, and cultivating a supportive community of learners contribute to a nurturing learning environment.

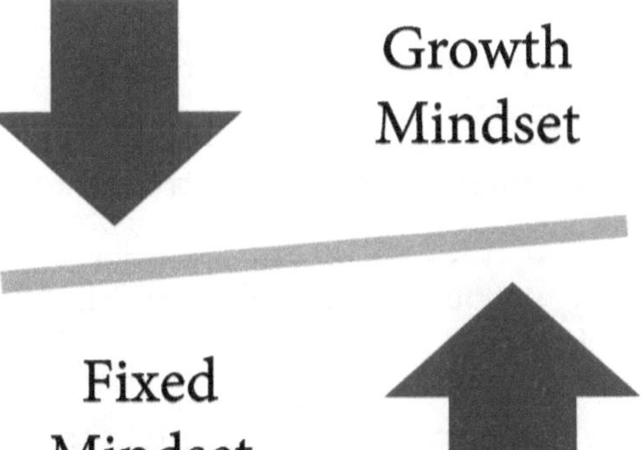

- Avoids challenges to maintain a sense of competence.
- Interprets failures as evidence of limited abilities and may give up easily.
- tributes success solely to innate abilities and intelligence.
- May be resistant to feedback and see it as a personal attack.

- Sees challenges as opportunities for learning and growth.
- Views setbacks as a chance to learn, adjust, and improve.
- Believes that success is achieved through effort and dedication.
- Welcomes feedback as an opportunity for growth and improvement.

Growth Mindset Self-Assessment

Instructions: Read each statement and indicate your level of agreement on a scale of 1 to 5, where 1 represents strongly disagree and 5 represents strongly agree.

Parameter	Score (1-5)
1. I believe that intelligence and abilities can be developed with effort and practice.	
2. I see challenges as opportunities to learn and grow.	
3. When faced with setbacks, I view them as temporary obstacles and not a reflection of my abilities.	
4. I enjoy learning new things and seeking out new knowledge.	
5. I believe that hard work and effort are necessary for achieving success.	
6. I am open to feedback and see it as a chance to improve and grow.	
7. I believe that talent alone is not enough; it is the effort that leads to mastery.	
8. I embrace failure as a valuable learning experience and use it as a stepping stone for growth.	
9. I see the value in stepping out of my comfort zone and taking on new challenges.	
10. I believe that my abilities can improve through deliberate practice and persistence.	

Scoring: Add up your scores for each statement to get your total score.

Interpreting your score

10-20: Low Growth Mindset: You may have a fixed mindset, believing that abilities are fixed and not easily changeable. Consider exploring strategies to cultivate a growth mindset.

21-30: Moderate Growth Mindset: You have some elements of a growth mindset but could benefit from further developing your beliefs in the power of effort and learning.

31-40: High Growth Mindset: You demonstrate a strong growth mindset, believing in the power of effort, learning, and continuous improvement.

Remember that this self-assessment provides a general indication and is not a definitive measure of your growth mindset. Use it as a starting point for self-reflection and consider exploring further resources and strategies to cultivate and strengthen your growth mindset.

There are several other more scientific tools available to measure and assess an individual's growth mindset. One commonly used tool is the Mindset Assessment Profile (MAP), developed by Carol Dweck and her colleagues. The MAP is a self-report questionnaire that measures an individual's beliefs about intelligence and growth mindset.

Another popular tool is the Growth Mindset Assessment, which is a series of statements or scenarios that individuals respond to, indicating their agreement or disagreement. The assessment provides insight into how individuals perceive their abilities and their beliefs about the malleability of intelligence.

Additionally, there are many online quizzes and surveys that can help you assess your own growth mindset. These tools often provide feedback and insights based on the responses given.

Developing a growth mindset can have significant long-term benefits for students as they navigate their educational journey and beyond. Here's an example illustrating how cultivating a growth mindset can contribute to long-term success:

Smriti, a first-year university student, initially held a fixed mindset, believing that her intelligence and abilities were predetermined. She approached her studies with caution, fearing failure and avoiding challenging tasks. However, Smriti's mindset began to transform as she encountered the concept of a growth mindset.

Inspired by the idea that intelligence can be developed through effort and effective strategies, Smriti decided to adopt a growth mindset. She recognised that challenges were opportunities for growth and embraced them with enthusiasm. Rather than shying away from difficult courses or assignments, she actively sought out intellectual challenges to expand her knowledge and skills.

Smriti's growth mindset led her to develop effective learning strategies. She sought guidance from professors, utilised online resources and educational platforms, and engaged in active learning techniques. She understood that success was not solely determined by innate talent but also by dedication, perseverance, and a willingness to learn from mistakes.

As Smriti progressed through her university journey, her growth mindset played a pivotal role in her long-term success. She approached her studies with a focus on continuous learning, consistently seeking opportunities to expand her understanding of her field. This mindset fuelled her curiosity and motivated her to explore research projects, participate in extracurricular activities, and collaborate with peers and professors. She utilised constructive feedback, analysed her mistakes, and adjusted her strategies accordingly. Her resilience and determination helped her overcome obstacles, maintain her motivation, and continue progressing towards her goals.

Beyond her university experience, Smriti's growth mindset extended to her personal and professional life. She embraced a lifelong learning mindset, staying updated with industry trends and seeking professional development opportunities. Her adaptability and willingness to learn allowed her to thrive in an ever-evolving job market and adapt to new roles and responsibilities.

CHAPTER 7

NAVIGATING THE JOB MARKET

Transitioning from higher education to the job market is a significant milestone in a student's journey towards professional success. It marks the culmination of years of hard work and learning, opening doors to exciting opportunities and challenges. However, this phase can also be daunting and overwhelming, as students face the need to make critical decisions that will shape their future careers. In this chapter, my aim is to provide comprehensive guidance on navigating the job market effectively, equipping students with the knowledge and tools they need to confidently step into the world of work.

THE FUTURE OF WORK

Rapid technological advancements, evolving workplace dynamics, and global trends are driving a profound shift in the job market. Automation, artificial intelligence, remote work, and the gig economy are just a few of the key factors revolutionising the way we approach employment. As we step into this dynamic future, embracing adaptability, continuous learning, and a keen understanding of emerging trends will be essential to thrive in the ever-evolving world of work.

THE GIG ECONOMY

The gig economy and freelancing have become significant phenomena in the modern workforce, transforming the way people work and how businesses operate.

The gig economy refers to a labour market characterised by the prevalence of short-term, freelance, or contract work rather than traditional, long-term employment. It is driven by digital platforms and marketplaces that connect individuals, often referred to as "gig workers", with businesses or clients seeking their services. These platforms provide a convenient and efficient way for gig workers to find work opportunities and for businesses to access specialised skills on demand. Digital platforms and connectivity have made it easier for individuals to work remotely, collaborate with clients or teams across borders, and market their services globally. This has created a borderless work environment, where geographical constraints are less relevant, and individuals can find work opportunities from anywhere in the world.

One of the key advantages of the gig economy is the flexibility it offers. Gig workers have the freedom to choose when, where, and how much they want to work. They can select projects or assignments that align with their skills, interests, and availability. This flexibility allows individuals to create a work-life balance that suits their needs, accommodating personal commitments, and pursuing other interests outside of work.

Freelancing platforms and digital marketplaces have played a pivotal role in facilitating the growth of the gig economy. These platforms provide a space where gig workers can showcase their skills, create professional profiles, and connect with potential clients. Examples of popular freelancing platforms include Upwork, Freelancer, and Fiverr. These platforms offer a diverse range of services, spanning from graphic design and content writing to software development and virtual assistance.

The gig economy and freelancing have reshaped traditional employment models by offering alternative ways of working. They have created opportunities for individuals to monetise their skills, even without formal employment contracts. This is particularly beneficial for those who prefer autonomy, control over their work, and the ability to explore different projects and industries.

For businesses, the gig economy provides access to a global talent pool, enabling them to tap into specialised skills and expertise on a project-by-project basis. It allows businesses to scale their workforce up or down based on their needs, without the long-term commitments associated with traditional employment. The gig economy also fosters innovation and agility, as businesses can quickly adapt to changing market demands by leveraging the skills and services available within the gig workforce.

However, the gig economy is not without its challenges. Gig workers often face uncertainty in terms of income stability, benefits, and long-term career progression. They may have to navigate issues such as managing multiple clients, securing consistent work, and dealing with payment disputes. It is crucial for gig workers to develop strong self-management skills, financial planning strategies, and a robust professional network to thrive in this dynamic work environment.

Despite these challenges, the gig economy offers unique opportunities for individuals to build diverse portfolios, explore different industries, and develop a broad range of skills. For many, gig work can serve as a stepping stone to entrepreneurship or even a full-time freelance career. It provides a platform to showcase skills, gain experience, and establish a reputation within specific niches or industries.

REMOTE WORK

The COVID-19 pandemic acted as a catalyst for the widespread adoption of remote work. In an effort to curb the spread of the virus, organisations worldwide had to quickly transition their employees to remote work arrangements. This forced experiment has demonstrated that remote work can be efficient, productive, and viable for many industries and job roles.

Remote work refers to a work arrangement where employees perform their tasks and responsibilities from a location outside of the traditional office environment. With advancements in technology and the availability of digital tools, remote work has become increasingly feasible and accessible. The ability to collaborate, communicate, and access work-related information remotely has enabled organisations to maintain business continuity during challenging times.

The adoption of remote work offers numerous benefits for both employees and employers. For employees, remote work provides flexibility in terms of work hours and location. It eliminates the need for commuting, reduces stress associated with transportation, and allows for a better work-life balance. Remote work also opens up possibilities for individuals living in remote areas or with personal circumstances that make traditional office work challenging.

Employers have also recognised the advantages of remote work. It can lead to increased productivity and employee satisfaction, as it eliminates office distractions and provides employees with a more comfortable and personalised work environment. Remote work also expands the talent pool for employers, as they can hire individuals from different geographical locations and access a diverse range of skills and perspectives.

According to Global Workplace Analytics (2021), remote work statistics reveal several significant findings. Before the pandemic, only a small percentage of the workforce worked remotely on a regular basis. However, as a result of the pandemic, remote work increased dramatically, with approximately 88% of organisations worldwide implementing remote work policies. Moreover, remote work is projected to continue with an estimated 25-30% of the workforce expected to work remotely multiple days per week in the coming future.

The benefits of remote work extend beyond the immediate crisis response. Remote work arrangements have the potential to reduce traffic congestion, lower pollution levels in large cities, and enhance work-life balance for employees. They also provide opportunities for cost savings for both employees and employers, such as reduced commuting expenses and office space requirements.

Remote work presents its own set of challenges, like maintaining effective communication and collaboration among team members who are physically dispersed. Leveraging technology tools and platforms, such as video conferencing and project management software, can help overcome these challenges by facilitating virtual interactions and seamless collaboration.

Another challenge is maintaining a work-life balance and setting boundaries between work and personal life. When working from home, it can be easy to blur the lines between work and personal time. Establishing a dedicated workspace, setting clear work hours, and maintaining regular breaks are important strategies to ensure a healthy work-life balance.

For remote work to be successful, organisations need to invest in supporting their remote workforce. This includes providing adequate technology infrastructure, promoting remote work best practices, and fostering a culture of trust and accountability. Managers play a crucial role in effectively leading remote teams, providing clear expectations, and maintaining open lines of communication.

UNDERSTANDING THE CURRENT JOB MARKET LANDSCAPE

To navigate the job market effectively, students must possess a deep understanding of the current employment landscape. This section aims to examine relevant statistics and trends, providing insights into industry growth sectors, job market demands, and emerging fields. By analysing this data, you can make informed decisions about your career paths and position yourself strategically to capitalise on potential opportunities.

INDUSTRY GROWTH SECTORS

Identifying industry growth sectors is essential for students seeking promising career prospects. By examining statistics and trends, you can gain insights into industries experiencing rapid expansion and demand for skilled professionals. For example:

a.   **Technology:** The technology sector has experienced an unprecedented surge in advancement and innovation over the past few years. With the digital revolution at its core, technological developments have reshaped industries, economies, and societies on a global scale. The implications of this rapid progress are substantial and are projected to have a profound impact on the job market in the coming years.

According to the Bureau of Labor Statistics, the demand for professionals in computer and information technology occupations is projected to grow at an impressive rate of 11% from 2020 to 2030. This growth rate surpasses the average for all occupations, underscoring the immense opportunities unfolding in the technology job market. As businesses and organisations increasingly rely on cutting-edge technologies, skilled professionals in this field become indispensable assets to drive efficiency, innovation, and competitiveness.

Several key factors drive this exponential growth in the technology job market. One significant driver is the widespread adoption of artificial intelligence (AI) across industries. AI, with its ability to process vast amounts of data, analyse patterns, and make autonomous decisions, is revolutionising industries ranging from healthcare and finance to manufacturing and transportation. The demand for AI experts, machine learning specialists, and data scientists is surging as organisations seek to harness the power of AI-driven insights and automation.

Moreover, the rising importance of cybersecurity cannot be overstated. As technology becomes more integrated into every aspect of modern life, the need for robust security measures intensifies. Cyber threats pose significant risks to businesses, governments, and individuals alike. Consequently, cybersecurity professionals, including ethical hackers and cybersecurity analysts, are in high demand to safeguard sensitive information and mitigate potential cyber-attacks.

Cloud computing is another pivotal area driving job market growth in technology. Organisations are shifting from traditional IT infrastructures to cloud-based solutions due to their scalability, cost-efficiency, and accessibility. Consequently, professionals with expertise in cloud computing, such as cloud architects and engineers, are sought after to manage and optimise cloud-based systems.

The rapid development of technologies like the Internet of Things (IoT), blockchain, and 5G connectivity also plays a significant role in reshaping the technology job market. These cutting-edge technologies have the potential to disrupt existing industries and create new ones, thereby creating a demand for skilled professionals capable of leveraging their potential.

b. **Healthcare:** The healthcare industry is one of the most dynamic and vital sectors, experiencing rapid growth and transformation fuelled by multiple factors. With an aging population and continuous advancements in medical technology, the demand for healthcare services and professionals is soaring, making it a promising and rewarding field for career opportunities.

In the United States, the U.S. Bureau of Labor Statistics projects that healthcare occupations will see the most substantial job growth from 2020 to 2030, adding a staggering 2.4 million jobs. This growth trajectory underscores the significant role healthcare plays in the nation's economy and the critical need for skilled healthcare professionals to meet the rising demands of an expanding population.

One of the primary drivers of growth in the healthcare job market is the aging population. As the baby boomer generation enters retirement age, there is a surge in the demand for healthcare services, particularly in areas like geriatric care and chronic disease management. This demographic shift creates a pressing need for healthcare professionals who specialise in providing personalised and compassionate care to the elderly.

Advancements in medical technology also play a pivotal role in the growth of the healthcare industry. Innovative medical devices, diagnostic tools, and treatment modalities are continuously being developed, revolutionising patient care and outcomes. The integration of telemedicine and digital health solutions has further expanded access to healthcare services, particularly in remote and underserved areas.

In India, similar trends are observed in the healthcare sector. The country's population is witnessing an increase in life expectancy, resulting in a larger elderly population in need of healthcare services. Additionally, the government's focus on enhancing healthcare infrastructure and accessibility has led to an increased demand for healthcare professionals across various disciplines.

In both the United States and India, nurses, physicians, and medical technologists are among the key healthcare occupations experiencing significant job growth. Nurses play a crucial role in patient care and are in high demand to address the increasing healthcare needs of diverse patient populations. Physicians, specialists, and general practitioners alike, are needed to cater to the varied healthcare requirements of the growing population. Medical technologists, on the other hand, are vital in conducting diagnostic tests, analysing results, and assisting physicians in accurate disease diagnosis and treatment.

Furthermore, healthcare job opportunities extend beyond direct patient care roles. The demand for healthcare administrators, healthcare IT professionals, and public health experts is also on the rise as organisations seek to streamline operations, improve healthcare systems, and address public health challenges.

c. **Healthcare Administration:** As the healthcare industry continues to experience remarkable expansion, there is an escalating demand for professionals possessing expertise in healthcare administration and management. Healthcare administrators play a pivotal role in overseeing the efficient functioning of healthcare facilities, managing budgets, and ensuring the seamless delivery of healthcare services.

One of the primary drivers behind the demand for healthcare administrators is the increasing complexity of healthcare systems. As medical technology advances and regulations evolve, healthcare facilities require skilled administrators who can navigate these complexities while ensuring compliance with changing guidelines and policies.

Moreover, the growing emphasis on healthcare efficiency and cost-effectiveness further underscores the need for competent healthcare administrators. These professionals are adept at managing budgets, controlling expenses, and optimising resource allocation, all of which are crucial for the financial sustainability of healthcare organisations.

In addition to overseeing day-to-day operations, healthcare administrators also play a key role in enhancing patient care outcomes. They collaborate with clinical staff to implement evidence-based practices, quality improvement initiatives, and patient safety protocols. By fostering a culture of continuous improvement and innovation, healthcare administrators contribute significantly to enhancing the overall quality of care provided to patients.

The growing trend of healthcare digitisation and the adoption of electronic health records (EHRs) have also increased the demand for healthcare administrators with a strong background in healthcare informatics and data management. These professionals are instrumental in leveraging technology to enhance data-driven decision-making, improve patient outcomes, and streamline administrative processes.

In India, the need for skilled healthcare administrators is also on the rise as the country strives to strengthen its healthcare infrastructure and delivery systems. The increasing focus on accessible and affordable healthcare services calls for proficient administrators who can efficiently manage healthcare facilities and resources to meet the needs of a diverse and expanding population.

Aspiring healthcare administrators should be equipped with a combination of healthcare knowledge, business acumen, and leadership skills. Pursuing advanced degrees in healthcare administration, healthcare management, or health services administration can provide the necessary education and training to excel in this rapidly growing field.

d. **Renewable Energy:** In response to the pressing need for sustainable solutions, the renewable energy sector has witnessed a surge in momentum and prominence. The International Renewable Energy Agency (IRENA) reports that, in 2020, the renewable energy industry employed over 12 million people worldwide, reflecting the growing demand for skilled professionals in diverse areas of renewable energy, including solar energy, wind power, and energy efficiency.

The global shift towards renewable energy is driven by several factors, including concerns about climate change, the depletion of fossil fuels, and the pursuit of energy independence. Renewable energy sources, such as solar, wind, hydro, geothermal, and biomass, offer environmentally friendly alternatives to conventional fossil fuels, contributing to a significant reduction in greenhouse gas emissions and combating the effects of climate change.

In the realm of solar energy, advancements in photovoltaic technology and a decline in solar panel costs have made solar power an increasingly viable and accessible energy option. As a result, there is a growing demand for professionals with expertise in designing, installing, and maintaining solar energy systems. Solar energy engineers, technicians, and project managers play crucial roles in harnessing the power of the sun to generate clean and sustainable electricity.

Wind power is another rapidly expanding sector within renewable energy. Advances in wind turbine technology, along with favourable policies promoting wind energy development, have propelled the growth of wind power projects worldwide. Wind energy specialists, wind farm managers, and maintenance technicians are in high demand to support the efficient and reliable operation of wind farms.

Energy efficiency has also emerged as a significant focus area within the renewable energy sector. Energy efficiency measures aim to optimise energy consumption while reducing waste and emissions. Professionals specialising in energy audits, building retrofitting, and energy management are instrumental in implementing energy-efficient practices across industries and residential spaces.

The demand for skilled professionals in renewable energy is not limited to developed countries; it extends globally, with emerging economies recognising the potential of renewables to address their energy needs sustainably. India, for instance, has been investing heavily in renewable energy projects, particularly solar and wind power. This has created a vast job market for renewable energy professionals, contributing to economic growth while reducing the country's carbon footprint.

The renewable energy sector offers a wide range of rewarding career opportunities for individuals passionate about sustainability and environmental conservation. Pursuing relevant education and training in renewable energy technologies, sustainable engineering, or energy management can equip individuals with the necessary skills to excel in this dynamic and rapidly evolving field.

e. **Environmental Science:** In the face of mounting global concerns about environmental degradation and the urgent need for sustainability, the field of environmental science has emerged as a critical and prominent discipline. Environmental scientists play a vital role in understanding and addressing a wide range of environmental issues, including climate change, pollution, habitat loss, and natural resource management.

The pressing challenges posed by climate change and its far-reaching consequences have put environmental science at the forefront of scientific research and policy discussions. Environmental scientists study the complex interactions between human activities and the natural environment, seeking solutions to mitigate the impacts of climate change and promote resilience in ecosystems.

Air and water pollution, caused by industrial activities, transportation, and agricultural practices, pose significant threats to human health and the environment. Environmental scientists analyse pollutant levels, assess their effects on ecosystems and human populations, and develop strategies to minimise pollution and protect the environment.

Conservation and natural resource management are also key focus areas within environmental science. With growing concerns about biodiversity loss and habitat destruction, environmental scientists work to preserve and restore ecosystems, protect endangered species, and ensure the sustainable use of natural resources for present and future generations.

The increasing awareness of the environmental impact of human activities has led both governments and businesses to prioritise sustainable practices and environmental compliance. As a result, the demand for professionals in environmental science is expected to grow significantly. Organisations across industries seek environmental scientists to conduct environmental assessments, develop sustainability strategies, and ensure adherence to environmental regulations.

Moreover, the push for sustainable development and responsible resource management has extended to emerging economies as well, creating a global demand for environmental science expertise. Countries like India, with their vast and diverse ecosystems, are recognising the importance of environmental conservation and sustainable practices, leading to a growing market for environmental science professionals.

A career in environmental science offers diverse and rewarding opportunities for individuals passionate about environmental protection and sustainability. Environmental scientists can work in various sectors, including government agencies, research institutions, non-governmental organisations (NGOs), consulting firms, and corporate sustainability departments.

For aspiring environmental scientists, pursuing a degree in environmental science or related fields such as ecology, environmental engineering, or natural resource management provides a strong foundation for a successful career. Additionally, acquiring specialised knowledge in areas like climate science, environmental policy, or environmental impact assessment can further enhance career prospects and enable professionals to make a meaningful impact in the field.

f. **E-Commerce & Digital Marketing:** The e-commerce and digital marketing sectors have witnessed significant growth on a global scale, driven by the increasing adoption of digital technologies and the growing preference for online shopping. The global e-commerce market was valued at USD 14.30 trillion in 2021 and reach USD 58.74 trillion by 2028, at a CAGR of 26.55% during the forecast period (2022-2028). This exponential growth reflects the increasing significance of e-commerce as a preferred mode of shopping for consumers worldwide.

The Indian e-commerce market was estimated to be worth over $55 billion in Gross Merchandise Value in 2021. By 2030, it is expected to have an annual gross merchandise value of $350 billion. Fuelling e-commerce growth, India is expected to have over 907 million internet users by 2023, which accounts for ~64% of the total population of the country. This tremendous growth is attributed to factors like a rise in disposable income, the convenience of online shopping, and the expansion of e-commerce platforms.

The rapid growth of e-commerce and digital marketing has created a demand for skilled professionals with expertise in digital marketing strategies, data analytics, and customer experience optimisation. Companies are seeking professionals who can leverage data insights to drive marketing decisions, target specific customer segments, and enhance overall customer experience.

Professionals with proficiency in search engine optimisation (SEO), search engine marketing (SEM), social media marketing, content marketing, and email marketing are highly sought after to craft effective digital marketing campaigns and enhance brand visibility.

Additionally, data analysts and data scientists are instrumental in interpreting customer data, conducting market research, and deriving actionable insights to optimise marketing efforts and improve customer engagement.

g.	**Education Technology (EdTech):** In recent years, the education sector in India has been experiencing a transformational shift with the integration of Education Technology, commonly known as EdTech. The advent of digital technologies and the increasing penetration of the internet have revolutionised the way education is delivered and accessed in the country. As a result, there is a significant surge in demand for EdTech professionals, instructional designers, and e-learning specialists who play pivotal roles in reshaping the landscape of education.

India has witnessed a remarkable rise in the number of EdTech start-ups catering to diverse educational needs. These start-ups are leveraging technology to offer interactive and engaging learning experiences, adaptive learning platforms, online tutoring, and test preparation courses. India's Edutech Market size was valued at US$ 1.45 billion in 2021 and revenue is expected to grow at 27.65% from 2022 to 2029, reaching nearly US$ 10.22 billion, signalling immense growth potential and opportunities in the sector.

The rise of Education Technology in India presents numerous opportunities for EdTech professionals, instructional designers, and e-learning specialists. With the increasing adoption of digital learning platforms, personalised learning experiences, and government support for digital education initiatives, the EdTech sector is poised for significant growth. As the education landscape continues to evolve, EdTech professionals will play a pivotal role in shaping the future of education in India, making learning more accessible, engaging, and effective for learners of all ages and backgrounds.

Among the sectors I have discussed, students can analyse data on the growth of various other industries to align their career aspirations and skill development with fields that present promising employment opportunities and long-term prospects for advancement.

Job Market Demands

Understanding job market demands is crucial for students to tailor their skills and qualifications to meet employer expectations. By analysing relevant data, students can gain insights into the skills and experiences that are in high demand. For example:

a. **Data Analysis:** The increasing volume of data in various industries has created a high demand for professionals with expertise in data analysis and interpretation. According to LinkedIn's 2021 Emerging Jobs Report, data science and analytics roles have seen significant growth, indicating the importance of skills such as statistical analysis, data visualisation, and machine learning.

b. **Digital Marketing:** The rise of digital platforms and online marketing has led to a surge in demand for professionals skilled in digital marketing strategies. According to a report by Burning Glass Technologies, digital marketing positions are projected to grow at a faster rate than the overall job market, emphasising the need for skills in search engine optimisation (SEO), social media marketing, and content creation.

c. **Cybersecurity:** With the increasing threat of cyber-attacks, the demand for cybersecurity professionals has soared. The U.S. Bureau of Labour Statistics projects a 31% growth rate for information security analyst positions from 2020 to 2030, highlighting the critical need for skills in cybersecurity management, ethical hacking, and risk assessment.

EMERGING FIELDS

Exploring emerging fields provides students with insights into industries that are poised for growth and transformation. By analysing data and trends, students can identify emerging fields that offer unique opportunities. For example:

a. **Blockchain Technology:** Blockchain technology has gained attention for its potential to revolutionise various industries, such as finance, supply chain management, and healthcare. According to a report by PwC, the global blockchain market is projected to reach $1.7 trillion by 2030, indicating substantial growth and demand for professionals with blockchain expertise.

b. **Virtual Reality (VR) and Augmented Reality (AR):** VR and AR technologies have expanded beyond gaming and entertainment, finding applications in fields like education, training, and marketing. The market for VR and AR is expected to reach $72.8 billion by 2024, according to Statista, highlighting the growing demand for professionals skilled in creating immersive experiences and developing virtual environments.

c. **Green Economy:** The shift towards sustainability has led to the emergence of the green economy, encompassing renewable energy, eco-friendly practices, and sustainable resource management. This field offers numerous opportunities for professionals focused on environmental conservation, green infrastructure development, and sustainable business practices.

Understanding the job market landscape equips students with a competitive edge, increasing their chances of success in securing rewarding careers and achieving long-term professional fulfilment.

CHAPTER 8

MANAGEMENT CONSULTING: CAREER OPPORTUNITIES

The reason behind my decision to craft a dedicated chapter on Management Consulting is rooted in my extensive experience, which has shown me that consulting roles are among the most sought after and coveted by most MBA students. It's a shared dream, a collective aspiration, to secure a position with a prestigious global consulting firm. Every time I engage with students discussing consulting careers, I can't help but notice the unmistakable twinkle in their eyes, the burning desire to excel in this field.

With this chapter, I aim to provide aspiring students with valuable insights into the consulting sector. I want to offer clarity, guidance, and a roadmap to help them better understand what it takes to succeed in this competitive arena.

Management consulting is a prestigious and dynamic career path that involves providing expert advice and solutions to organisations across various industries. Consultants work on a diverse range of projects, assisting clients in solving complex business challenges, optimising processes, and driving strategic growth. As management consultants, individuals get the opportunity to work with top-tier clients, tackle challenging problems, and make a significant impact on the success of businesses.

COMPANIES IN THE MANAGEMENT CONSULTING SPACE

Several renowned companies operate in the management consulting space, offering diverse services and expertise. Some of the prominent global and Indian management consulting firms include:

Global Consulting Firms

- McKinsey & Company
- Boston Consulting Group (BCG)
- Bain & Company
- Deloitte Consulting
- PwC (PricewaterhouseCoopers) Consulting
- Accenture
- EY (Ernst & Young) Advisory Services
- KPMG Advisory

Indian Consulting Firms

- Tata Consultancy Services (TCS) Consulting
- Infosys Consulting
- Wipro Consulting Services
- HCL Consulting
- KPMG India Advisory
- Deloitte India Advisory
- EY India Advisory

JOB ROLES IN MANAGEMENT CONSULTING

Management consulting firms offer various job roles with increasing levels of responsibility and expertise. Some common job roles in management consulting include:

- **Business Analyst:** Entry-level role involving data analysis, research, and report preparation.

- **Associate Consultant:** Supporting senior consultants in project execution, data analysis, and client interactions.

- **Consultant:** Leading project workstreams, analysing data, and contributing to strategic recommendations.

- **Senior Consultant:** Managing project teams, overseeing client engagements, and delivering strategic solutions.

- **Manager:** Leading project teams, driving business development, and building client relationships.

- **Principal/Senior Manager:** Managing multiple projects, driving thought leadership, and managing client accounts.
- **Partner/Director:** Providing overall strategic direction, leading business development efforts, and managing client relationships.

SKILLS REQUIRED

Management consulting firms seek candidates with a blend of analytical, problem-solving, and interpersonal skills. Some essential skills required to join these companies include:

- **Analytical Skills:** Ability to analyse complex data, draw insights, and make data-driven recommendations.
- **Problem-Solving:** Strong problem-solving abilities to address diverse business challenges.
- **Communication:** Effective communication and presentation skills to convey findings and recommendations clearly.
- **Collaboration:** Capacity to work collaboratively in teams, including cross-functional and client teams.
- **Adaptability:** Flexibility to handle dynamic project environments and learn quickly on the job.
- **Leadership:** Leadership potential and the ability to take ownership of projects and deliver results.
- **Industry Knowledge:** An understanding of industry trends and business dynamics is beneficial.

SALARIES IN INR*

Salaries in management consulting vary based on factors such as experience, educational background, and the consulting firm's reputation. Approximate salary ranges in INR for some entry-level roles are as follows:

---

* Salaries may vary

- **Business Analyst:** 8 to 14 lakhs per annum
- **Associate Consultant:** 12 to 18 lakhs per annum
- **Consultant:** 15 to 25 lakhs per annum

Management consulting firms actively recruit from top-tier business schools and universities. Additionally, they also consider candidates with relevant industry experience and exceptional skills. Many firms conduct summer internships and campus placements to hire fresh talent.

Career progression in management consulting typically involves moving up the ranks from entry-level roles to leadership positions like Partner or Director. The advancement often depends on performance, expertise, and business development skills. Some professionals may choose to specialise in specific industries or functional areas.

PREPARING FOR INTERVIEWS

Preparing for management consulting interviews requires a multifaceted approach:

- **Case Interviews:** Practice solving case studies to demonstrate problem-solving skills and analytical abilities.
- **Industry Knowledge:** Stay updated on industry trends and the specific sectors of interest to the consulting firm.
- **Behavioural Questions:** Be ready to answer behavioural questions that assess teamwork, leadership, and communication skills.
- **Mock Interviews:** Conduct mock interviews with peers or professionals to receive feedback and improve performance.
- **Networking:** Build connections with professionals in the consulting industry to gain insights and potential referrals.

DIFFERENT LAYERS OF INTERVIEWS

The interview process in management consulting typically involves multiple rounds:

1. **Resume Screening:** Initial screening based on the candidate's resume and qualifications.

2. **Case Interview:** A common feature in consulting interviews, candidates are presented with business scenarios and expected to propose solutions.

3. **Behavioural Interview:** Assessing the candidate's soft skills, teamwork, leadership, and problem-solving approach.

4. **Fit Interview:** Evaluating the candidate's fit with the company's culture and values.

5. **Partner/Principal Interview:** Final interview with senior leadership to assess the candidate's potential as a long-term fit for the firm.

OTHER IMPORTANT DETAILS

Travel: Management consultants often travel for client engagements, varying based on the firm and project.

Work-Life Balance: The workload in management consulting can be demanding, requiring commitment and time management.

Training and Development: Consulting firms invest in training and development programmes to upskill their consultants continuously.

Certifications: Some firms may value certifications like Six Sigma or PMP, depending on the focus of their projects.

Exit Opportunities: Management consulting provides a strong foundation for diverse career paths, including entrepreneurship, corporate leadership, or specialised consulting.

FUTURE OF CONSULTING JOBS IN INDIA

The future of consulting jobs in India appears to be promising, driven by several factors that are shaping the industry. However, please note that the consulting landscape is subject to continuous change and development. For the most current and accurate information, I recommend referring to recent reports, industry analysis, and consulting firms' official statements.

POTENTIAL TRENDS AND OUTLOOK FOR CONSULTING JOBS IN INDIA

- **Digital Transformation:** The demand for consulting services related to digital transformation was expected to grow. As organisations increasingly embraced digital technologies, consultants played a vital role in guiding them through the digitalisation process.

- **Data Analytics and AI:** The use of data analytics and artificial intelligence (AI) was gaining prominence across industries. Consultants proficient in data-driven decision-making and AI implementation were likely to be in high demand.

- **Sustainability Consulting:** With a growing focus on environmental sustainability and corporate social responsibility, consulting firms that offered expertise in sustainable practices were anticipated to see increased opportunities.

- **Healthcare and Life Sciences:** The healthcare and life sciences sectors were projected to witness significant consulting demand due to rapid advancements, regulatory changes, and the need for operational improvements.

- **E-commerce and Start-ups:** India's thriving e-commerce ecosystem and start-up culture offered opportunities for consultants to support new ventures and established players in strategising for growth and market expansion.

- **Government Initiatives:** The Indian government's emphasis on initiatives like "Make in India" and "Digital India" could create consulting opportunities for firms specialising in policy advisory and project implementation.

Hiring Trends in Consulting

While specific hiring trends may vary across different consulting firms and industries, some general observations regarding consulting job recruitment are prevalent:

- **Campus Placements:** Top-tier consulting firms actively participated in campus recruitment drives at leading business schools and engineering colleges to hire fresh talent.

- **Virtual Hiring:** After the COVID-19 pandemic, virtual interviews and remote onboarding processes are still common, making it more accessible for candidates from different regions to apply for consulting roles.

- **Diverse Skill Sets:** Firms increasingly look for candidates with diverse skill sets, including data analysis, programming, and domain-specific knowledge, to cater to the evolving needs of clients.

- **Focus on Soft Skills:** In addition to technical proficiency, consulting firms value candidates with strong communication, leadership, and client-facing skills.

- **Specialisation:** Some consulting firms show great interest in hiring specialists with expertise in specific industries or functional areas to strengthen their offerings in niche markets.

It's important to understand that the consulting job market is influenced by economic conditions, industry trends, and geopolitical factors. To stay updated on the latest hiring trends and developments in the consulting industry in India, please do consider referring to credible sources such as industry reports, consulting firm websites, and business publications. Additionally, networking with professionals in the field and attending industry events can provide valuable insights into the current state of consulting jobs in India.

CHAPTER 9

JOB SEARCH STRATEGIES FOR THE FUTURE

As students in higher education, preparing for the job market of the future requires a proactive and forward-thinking approach. The traditional methods of job searching are evolving rapidly, driven by technological advancements and changing employer expectations. To stand out in a competitive landscape, students need to adopt innovative strategies that align with the future job market's demands. In this chapter, we will explore effective job search strategies specifically tailored for students in higher education. From leveraging digital branding and networking to embracing remote work and continuous learning, these tactics will empower students to navigate the future job market successfully while still pursuing their education.

1. **Digital Branding and Online Presence:**

   In the digital era, building a compelling online presence and personal brand is essential for students. Creating a professional LinkedIn profile and showcasing academic achievements, projects, and extracurricular activities can demonstrate a student's skills and potential to potential employers. Engaging in industry-related discussions and sharing thought leadership can also position students as proactive and knowledgeable candidates.

2. **Networking and Building Connections:**

Networking is a powerful tool for students seeking future job opportunities. Engaging with alumni, professors, industry professionals, and fellow students can open doors to internships, mentorship, and valuable insights into career paths. Attending virtual events, webinars, and conferences can expand the network and provide exposure to diverse career opportunities.

3. **Utilising Career Services and Internships:**

Higher education institutions often offer career services that provide guidance on resume building, interview preparation, and job searching. Students should actively utilise these resources to enhance their employability. Participating in internships or cooperative education programmes can also provide real-world experience, build connections, and increase the chances of securing a full-time job post-graduation.

4. **Remote Work and Freelancing:**

The future job market is likely to embrace remote work and freelancing opportunities. Students can gain a competitive edge by exploring virtual internships or freelance projects related to their field of study. Embracing remote work opportunities during higher education allows students to demonstrate adaptability and effective time management skills.

5. **Continuous Learning and Skill Development:**

In a rapidly evolving job market, continuous learning is vital. Students should take advantage of online courses, workshops, and certifications to acquire new skills and stay up-to-date with industry trends. Highlighting relevant skills and certifications on resumes can make students more appealing to employers seeking adaptable and proactive candidates.

6. **Personalising Job Applications and Internship Outreach:**

Generic job applications and internship outreach emails often yield limited results. Students should tailor their application materials to match the specific requirements of each opportunity. Demonstrating a genuine interest in the company's mission and values can make a strong impression on potential employers.

Navigating the job market of the future requires a strategic and proactive approach. As the job market continues to evolve, students who stay ahead of the curve and adapt to changing trends will position themselves for rewarding and fulfilling career opportunities upon graduation.

BUILDING YOUR PROFESSIONAL BRAND

Building a powerful professional brand is crucial for students as they enter the job market and seek to establish themselves in their desired careers. By developing a strong personal brand, students can differentiate themselves from the competition, showcase their unique strengths, and attract great opportunities. Here are key points on how building a professional brand can help students succeed in the job market:

a. **Differentiation and Visibility:**

Crafting a personal brand allows you to stand out in a competitive job market. By defining your unique value proposition, strengths, and areas of expertise, you can differentiate yourself from others with similar qualifications. This helps potential employers recognise and remember you among numerous applicants.

b. **Establishing Credibility and Expertise:**

A strong personal brand helps establish credibility and positions you as an expert in your chosen field. By consistently sharing valuable insights, demonstrating thought leadership, and showcasing your skills and experiences, you can build a reputation as a knowledgeable professional.

c. **Networking and Connections:**

Your well-crafted personal brand facilitates networking and expands your professional connections. By leveraging online platforms, attending industry events, and actively engaging with professionals in your field, you can develop meaningful relationships and access a wider network of contacts. These connections can provide mentorship, guidance, job referrals, and other valuable career opportunities.

d. **Enhancing Job Search Efforts:**

A strong personal brand positively impacts your job search efforts. When employers recognise your brand, they may proactively reach out with job opportunities or consider you for roles that align with your brand identity. Additionally, an established personal brand increases the likelihood of being found by recruiters and hiring managers who are actively searching for candidates with specific expertise or skills.

e. **Building Trust and Authenticity:**

Your well-crafted personal brand allows you to showcase your authenticity, values, and personality. By sharing your genuine experiences, passions, and stories, you can build trust with potential employers. Employers often seek candidates who align with their company culture and values, and a strong personal brand helps convey that alignment.

f. **Career Growth and Long-term Success:**

Building a powerful professional brand sets the stage for long-term career growth and success. As you continue to develop your brand, gain experience, and refine your skills, you become recognised as a trusted professional in your industry. This opens doors to exciting opportunities, promotions, collaborations, and leadership roles.

Remember, crafting your personal brand is a continuous process. Be intentional in defining your unique identity, consistently communicate your strengths, and stay authentic in your interactions.

TIPS FOR BUILDING A POWERFUL PROFESSIONAL BRAND

- **Define Your Unique Value Proposition:** Identify your strengths, skills, and unique qualities that set you apart from others. Understand your target audience and the value you can provide to them.

- **Craft a Compelling Personal Brand Statement:** Create a concise statement that communicates your expertise, values, and the unique value you bring to the table.

- **Develop a Strong Online Presence:** Build a professional website or online portfolio to showcase your work, accomplishments, and expertise. Optimise your LinkedIn profile to reflect your brand consistently.

- **Share Valuable Content:** Create and share valuable content related to your field of expertise. This can include articles, blog posts, videos, or infographics that showcase your knowledge and insights.

- **Engage with Your Network:** Actively participate in industry-related discussions, join relevant groups, and network with professionals in your field. Engage in conversations, offer insights, and build relationships.

- **Seek Feedback and Continuously Improve:** Request feedback from mentors, colleagues, or industry professionals to gain insights into your personal brand. Continuously learn, grow, and adapt to stay relevant in your field.

By building a powerful professional brand, students can establish themselves in the job market, attract desirable opportunities, and forge a successful career path. It requires consistency, authenticity, and a commitment to showcasing their unique strengths and expertise to potential employers and industry peers.

OPTIMISE YOUR LINKEDIN PROFILE

Optimising your online professional profiles, particularly on platforms like LinkedIn, is vital for attracting the attention of potential employers in the digital job market. To make the most of your online presence, consider the following tips:

a.   **Craft a Captivating Headline:**

Your headline is one of the first things employers see, so make it engaging and informative. Use keywords relevant to your desired role or industry to attract attention and showcase your expertise.

b.   **Write a Concise yet Impactful Summary:**

In your profile summary, provide a concise overview of your professional background, highlighting your key accomplishments, skills, and career goals. Use industry-specific keywords and power words to make a strong impression and pique the interest of employers.

Here's an example of a concise and impactful LinkedIn professional summary of a Biotechnology final-year student:

As a final-year Biotechnology student with a passion for cutting-edge research and innovation, I am driven to make a lasting impact in the field of life sciences. Equipped with a strong foundation in molecular biology, genetics, and bioinformatics, I am eager to apply my knowledge and skills to address real-world challenges. Throughout my academic journey, I have actively engaged in laboratory projects and collaborated with diverse teams, honing my analytical and problem-solving abilities. Seeking opportunities to contribute to ground-breaking discoveries and advancements in biotechnology, I am committed to fostering a sustainable and healthier future for all. Let's connect and explore how we can drive innovation together.

c. **Highlight Relevant Skills and Experiences:**

Feature your skills and experiences prominently, emphasising those that align with your career objectives. Showcase your expertise, certifications, and accomplishments to demonstrate your capabilities to potential employers.

d. **Utilise a Professional Profile Photo:**

Choose a high-quality, professional-looking profile photo that presents you in a positive and approachable light. Dress appropriately for your industry and ensure the background is clean and uncluttered.

e. **Seek Recommendations and Endorsements:**

Request recommendations from colleagues, supervisors, or professors who can speak to your skills and work ethic. These recommendations provide social proof of your capabilities and can greatly enhance your profile's credibility. Additionally, seek endorsements for specific skills to further validate your expertise.

f. **Engage in Thoughtful Content Sharing:**

Share relevant industry articles, insights, or your own content to demonstrate your knowledge and engagement in your field. Engage with others' posts by commenting and offering valuable input to establish yourself as a thought leader and expand your professional network.

g. **Customise Your URL:**

Personalise your profile's URL to make it more professional and memorable. This allows you to easily share your profile with others and optimise your online presence. E.g.: www.linkedin.com/in/ajaykhanna

h. **Join Relevant Professional Groups:**

Become an active participant in professional groups related to your industry. Engage in discussions, share valuable insights, and connect with professionals who share similar interests and career aspirations. For example, 'Job Seekers', a group for career networking, interview tips, and job opportunities

i. **Network Strategically:**

Utilise LinkedIn's networking capabilities to connect with professionals in your desired field. Personalise connection requests with a brief introduction or explanation of why you are interested in connecting. Cultivate meaningful relationships with individuals who can offer guidance, mentorship, or potential job opportunities.

j. **Regularly Update and Maintain Your Profile:**

Consistently update your profile with new experiences, achievements, and skills. Stay active by sharing relevant content, engaging with others, and responding to messages and connection requests in a timely manner.

Building a strong network on LinkedIn is essential to enhance your career prospects and create meaningful connections within your chosen industry. Here are my four top tips on how you can build your network on LinkedIn:

1. **Connect with Classmates and Professors:** Start by connecting with your classmates and professors. Building relationships within your university community lays a strong foundation for networking and can lead to potential opportunities, recommendations, or referrals.

2. **Leverage Alumni Networks:** Many universities have active alumni networks on LinkedIn. Reach out to alumni working in your desired industry or companies of interest. Join alumni groups to access a broader network of professionals who share a common educational background.

3. **Personalise Connection Invitations:** When sending connection invitations, personalise your messages instead

of using the default text. Mention shared interests, common connections, or any specific reason for connecting to show genuine interest.

4. **Follow Companies and Influencers:** Follow companies of interest and industry influencers to stay updated on their latest developments and insights. Engage with their content and comment thoughtfully to get noticed.

How Does LinkedIn Algorithm Work?

LinkedIn's algorithm is a complex system that uses various factors to determine what content appears in a user's LinkedIn feed. It is designed to show users content that is most relevant and engaging to them. Here's how it works and how it can benefit job seekers and students:

1. **Personalised Content:** The LinkedIn algorithm takes into account a user's activity and preferences. It considers the type of content a user engages with (likes, comments, shares), their connections, and the industries they are interested in. It then uses this data to personalise the content in the user's feed.

2. **Engagement Metrics:** LinkedIn values content that generates high engagement. Posts with more likes, comments, and shares are more likely to be shown to a wider audience. This encourages users to create high-quality content that resonates with their network.

3. **Relevancy:** The algorithm aims to show users content that is relevant to their professional interests and goals. For job seekers and students, this means they are more likely to see posts related to job openings, career advice, industry trends, and educational opportunities.

4. **Network Activity:** The algorithm also considers the activity of a user's connections. If a user's connections engage with a particular post or share content related to job opportunities,

it may appear in the user's feed, increasing visibility for job seekers.

5.	**Virality:** Content that has the potential to go viral is favoured by the algorithm. If a post starts to gain traction quickly, LinkedIn may show it to a broader audience, which can be beneficial for job seekers looking to network or students seeking exposure.

As I end this chapter, I want to reiterate that, networking on LinkedIn is not just about seeking immediate benefits; it's about building genuine and long-lasting relationships. Be authentic, respectful, and proactive in maintaining your connections. By investing time and effort into building your LinkedIn network, you can open doors to exciting opportunities and career growth throughout your university journey and beyond.

CHAPTER 10

THE ROLE OF MENTORS AND SUPPORT NETWORKS

Amidst the bustling campuses of higher education, where dreams take root and knowledge blossoms, a quiet force exerts its profound influence: mentors. These mentors are the unsung heroes, the architects of dreams, and the beacons of guidance for countless students. Let me introduce you to a real-life example that vividly illustrates the transformative power of mentorship in the Indian context.

Meet Jagriti, an ambitious undergraduate student, navigating the intricate maze of academic choices and career aspirations. The path ahead was daunting, filled with uncertainties and challenges. In this crucial phase of her educational journey, Jagriti crossed paths with Dr. Gupta, a seasoned professor known for nurturing talent. Their connection was more than just academic; it was a lifeline for Jagriti's dreams.

The role of mentors and support networks is paramount. The guidance and support provided by mentors can be transformative, helping you navigate challenges, make informed decisions, and unlock your full potential. Additionally, building strong professional networks and forming meaningful relationships within one's chosen field can open doors to opportunities, insights, and valuable connections. This chapter explores the significance of mentors, career coaches and support networks, delving into the benefits of coaching and mentorship programmes, and professional relationships. By understanding how to choose a mentor, what to expect in a mentoring programme, and the distinction between a mentor and a coach, you can tap into the power of the support networks to accelerate your personal and professional growth.

Benefits of Having a Mentor:

a. **Valuable Guidance:** Mentors offer valuable guidance based on their own experiences and expertise. They provide insights and advice that you may not have access to otherwise, helping you navigate challenges and make informed decisions.

b. **Goal Setting:** Mentors assist students in setting goals and creating actionable plans to achieve them. They help you identify your strengths, weaknesses, and areas of improvement, and provide guidance on how to maximise your potential.

c. **Encouragement and Support:** Mentors offer encouragement and support throughout the student's journey. They provide a safe space for you to share your aspirations, fears, and challenges while offering motivation and reassurance.

d. **Constructive Feedback:** Mentors provide constructive feedback to help students grow and develop. They offer insights into areas for improvement, suggest alternative approaches, and help you learn from your mistakes.

e. **Networking Opportunities:** Mentors often have extensive professional networks, which they can leverage to create networking opportunities for students. They may introduce you to industry professionals, connect you with internship or job opportunities, or provide recommendations.

f. **Role Models:** Mentors act as role models, inspiring students through their own achievements, work ethic, and values. By observing your mentors' success and professional conduct, you can learn valuable lessons and emulate their positive qualities.

g. **Accountability:** Mentors hold students accountable for their actions and goals. They help you stay focused, motivated, and committed to your personal and professional growth. Mentors provide a sense of responsibility and encourage students to take ownership of their actions.

h. **Expanded Perspectives:** Mentors offer different perspectives and insights that broaden students' horizons. They challenge you to think critically, consider alternative viewpoints, and explore new ideas, fostering intellectual growth.

i. **Emotional Support:** Mentors provide emotional support and serve as a trusted confidant. They offer guidance during challenging times, helping you overcome obstacles and build resilience.

j. **Long-term Relationships:** Mentorship often extends beyond the immediate academic or career context. Mentors can become lifelong advisers and advocates, providing ongoing guidance and support as you navigate your professional journeys.

TIPS FOR CHOOSING A MENTOR

Choosing the right mentor is a crucial step in establishing a successful mentoring relationship. By considering factors such as expertise, compatibility, and diversity, students can find mentors who provide the guidance and support they need to excel in their educational and professional endeavours.

a. **Identify Your Goals and Needs**: Before seeking a mentor, take the time to identify your goals, aspirations, and areas where you need guidance. This self-reflection will help you find a mentor who aligns with your specific needs.

b. **Look for Expertise and Experience:** Seek mentors who have expertise and experience in your field of interest. Consider their professional accomplishments, industry knowledge, and track record of success. A mentor with relevant experience can provide valuable insights and guidance.

c. **Compatibility and Chemistry:** Look for compatibility and chemistry with potential mentors. A strong mentor-mentee relationship is built on trust, mutual respect, and effective communication. Consider factors such as communication styles, values, and personality traits that align with your own.

d. **Seek Diversity:** Consider mentors from diverse backgrounds who can offer different perspectives and broaden your horizons. Diversity in mentorship can expose you to a range of experiences, ideas, and approaches that enrich your learning and personal growth.

e. **Seek Constructive Criticism:** Look for a mentor who is willing to provide honest feedback and constructive criticism. A mentor who challenges your thinking and pushes you outside your comfort zone can spur personal and professional growth.

f. **Establish Mutually Beneficial Expectations:** Clarify expectations and goals with your potential mentor. Discuss the frequency and mode of communication, the duration of the mentoring relationship, and the specific areas where you seek guidance. Ensure that both parties have a clear understanding of what they can offer and expect from the mentorship.

g. **Seek Mentors from Various Sources:** Explore different avenues to find mentors. Besides professional connections, consider reaching out to alumni networks, professional associations, or mentoring programmes offered by educational institutions or industry organisations. These sources can provide access to mentors with diverse experiences and perspectives.

h. **Maintain Professionalism and Respect:** When approaching potential mentors, demonstrate professionalism, respect, and gratitude. Clearly articulate why you believe they would be a valuable mentor and express your enthusiasm for learning from them.

i. **Build the Relationship Gradually:** Once you have identified a mentor, build the relationship gradually. Start with small interactions, seek their advice on specific topics, and demonstrate your commitment to their guidance. As the relationship grows, you can explore deeper mentoring conversations and seek broader guidance.

SETTING EXPECTATIONS IN A MENTORING PROGRAMME

By setting clear and realistic expectations in a mentoring programme, both mentors and mentees can work together effectively towards shared goals. Open communication, mutual understanding, and ongoing feedback are essential for maintaining a productive and meaningful mentoring relationship.

a. **Define Your Goals:** Clearly define your goals and areas of focus for the mentoring programme. Consider what you hope to achieve, whether it's acquiring specific skills, gaining industry insights, or navigating career decisions. Communicate these goals to your mentor to ensure alignment.

b. **Be Specific:** When discussing expectations, be specific about what you hope to gain from the mentoring programme. Provide examples or scenarios to help your mentor understand your needs and areas where you seek guidance. This specificity will help both parties work towards actionable outcomes.

c. **Establish a Schedule:** Determine the frequency and duration of mentoring sessions. Agree on a schedule that works for both you and your mentor. Establishing regular meetings or check-ins ensures consistent communication and progress towards your goals.

d. **Determine Preferred Modes of Communication:** Discuss and agree upon the preferred modes of communication for mentoring interactions. Whether it's face-to-face meetings, phone calls, video conferences, or email exchanges, find the communication methods that work best for both you and your mentor.

e. **Clarify Availability:** Understand each other's availability and set expectations regarding response times. Mentors may have other commitments, so it's important to establish realistic expectations for communication and availability. Find a balance that respects both parties' time constraints.

f. **Open and Honest Communication:** Foster an environment of open and honest communication. Encourage feedback and be receptive to suggestions from your mentor. Regularly communicate your progress, challenges, and any changes in your goals or needs.

g. **Guidance and Support:** Clearly express your expectations for guidance and support from your mentor. Discuss the level of involvement you desire, whether it's advice on specific projects, career guidance, or broader insights into the industry. Your mentor can provide valuable support tailored to your needs.

h. **Confidentiality:** Address any concerns regarding confidentiality upfront. Mentoring relationships often involve sharing personal and professional information. Ensure that both you and your mentor are committed to maintaining confidentiality and respecting each other's privacy.

i. **Review and Revise:** Periodically review and revise your expectations as your needs evolve. Regularly assess whether your goals and expectations are being met and communicate any adjustments or changes to your mentor.

j. **Express Gratitude:** Show appreciation and gratitude for your mentor's guidance and support. Recognise the time and effort they invest in your development. Regularly express your thanks to maintain a positive and mutually beneficial mentoring relationship.

COACHING OR MENTORING?

Coaching and mentoring are both effective approaches that can support students in their personal and professional development. The choice between coaching and mentoring depends on the specific goals and needs of the student.

Coaching is typically focused on specific skills development, performance enhancement, and behaviour change. It is particularly useful when students have identified specific areas they want to improve or skills they want to develop. Coaches provide structured guidance, feedback, and support, using specific methodologies and frameworks to help students achieve their goals. Coaching is effective for targeted skill acquisition, such as public speaking, leadership development, or time management. It offers a structured approach to accelerate growth and achieve specific outcomes.

On the other hand, mentoring offers a more holistic approach that draws on the mentor's experiences, knowledge, and wisdom. Mentors provide guidance, support, and advice based on their own professional journeys and can assist students in navigating their overall career paths. Mentoring relationships often involve a long-term commitment, focusing on personal and professional growth, goal setting, and overall development. Mentors offer insights, share experiences, and act as trusted advisers. Mentoring is particularly valuable when students seek guidance in areas such as career exploration, networking, decision-making, and professional growth.

The choice between coaching and mentoring ultimately depends on the student's goals, needs, and preferences. Some students may benefit from a structured coaching approach to enhance specific skills, while others may find long-term guidance and support from a mentor more valuable. In some cases, students may even choose to engage in both coaching and mentoring relationships simultaneously, as each approach offers unique benefits.

It is important for students to consider their individual goals, desired outcomes, and the areas in which they seek support. They should reflect on whether they require targeted skill development or comprehensive guidance in navigating their overall career paths. By understanding the distinctions between coaching and mentoring and considering their specific needs, students can make an informed decision and choose the approach that best aligns with their goals and aspirations.

PEER SUPPORT & COLLABORATIONS

Peer support and collaboration are vital components of a student's educational journey, offering numerous benefits that extend beyond the classroom. The power of peer relationships lies in the sense of camaraderie and shared experiences that they cultivate. When students come together, they form a supportive network that fuels their academic and personal growth.

One of the primary ways peer support manifests is through collaboration on group projects. Working together on assignments allows students to combine their unique perspectives, skills, and expertise. By pooling your knowledge, you can tackle complex problems more effectively and gain insights that may not have been apparent individually. Collaborative projects also teach valuable teamwork and communication skills, preparing students for future professional settings where collaboration is essential.

In addition to group projects, students can collaborate through study sessions. Studying with peers provides a structured environment for focused learning, where students can quiz each other, clarify doubts, and reinforce understanding. This interactive approach to learning helps solidify concepts, making it easier to retain information and perform better academically.

Extracurricular activities, whether in clubs, sports teams, or volunteering initiatives, also offer opportunities for peer collaboration. Engaging in these activities enables you to bond over shared interests and passions, creating a sense of community and belonging.

Moreover, peer support extends beyond academics and extracurriculars. Students often face personal challenges and stress during their educational journey. Having a network of supportive peers can be immensely beneficial during tough times.

The exchange of ideas and knowledge among peers contributes to an intellectually stimulating environment. Students can engage in lively discussions, challenge each other's viewpoints, and broaden their horizons through exposure to diverse perspectives. This fosters critical thinking and enhances their overall learning experience.

Engaging with Faculty & Professors

Engaging with professors and faculty members is a valuable aspect of a student's academic journey, offering a wealth of opportunities and advantages. Building strong relationships with these educators can lead to a more enriching educational experience and open doors to various prospects beyond the classroom.

Professors and faculty members possess a wealth of knowledge and experience in their respective fields. By actively participating in class discussions, students have the chance to tap into this expertise and gain valuable insights beyond what is covered in textbooks.

Attending office hours is another way students can connect with their professors on a more personal level. During these one-on-one sessions, students can seek clarification on complex topics, discuss their academic goals, and explore potential research opportunities or career paths. Professors often appreciate the initiative shown by students who take the time to attend office hours, and it can lead to a deeper understanding of course material and a more supportive learning environment.

Seeking feedback from professors on academic performance is a proactive way to improve and grow as a student. By soliciting constructive criticism, students can identify areas of improvement and receive valuable advice on how to excel in their studies. This feedback loop fosters continuous learning and encourages students to strive for excellence in their academic pursuits.

Moreover, developing strong relationships with professors can lead to mentorship opportunities. Some educators are willing to take on mentoring roles, offering guidance and support beyond the academic realm. Mentorship from a professor can be invaluable in terms of professional development, career advice, and navigating the complexities of higher education.

The relationships built during higher education can have a lasting impact on a student's personal and professional growth, shaping their path to success in both their educational pursuits and future endeavours beyond the classroom.

ALUMNI SUPPORT NETWORK

Networking with alumni is a strategic move that can greatly benefit current students during their higher education journey and beyond. University alumni serve as a valuable resource, offering a wealth of experience, insights, and connections that can enhance a student's academic and professional pursuits.

One of the primary ways you can connect with alumni is through networking events organised by the university or alumni associations. These events provide an opportunity for students to meet and interact with alumni from various industries and career paths. Engaging in these events allows students to learn from the experiences of those who have navigated similar academic journeys and entered the workforce successfully.

Alumni often willingly share their experiences and knowledge with current students, offering valuable career advice and industry insights. Their first-hand experiences can provide unique perspectives and help students make informed decisions about their own career paths. Alumni may also be able to offer guidance on specific career fields, potential job opportunities, and the skills and qualifications sought by employers.

Alumni networks can serve as a bridge between the academic world and the professional world. Some universities have established formal mentoring programmes that pair current students with alumni mentors. These mentorship opportunities allow students to receive personalised guidance, support, and feedback from seasoned professionals who have walked a similar path.

Chapter 11

Overcoming Common Challenges

In the pursuit of higher education, students often encounter a myriad of challenges that can be both daunting and discouraging. However, it is essential to remember that overcoming these obstacles is a natural part of the learning and personal growth process. In this chapter, we will explore some of the common challenges that students face during their higher education journey and provide practical advice on how to conquer them. By understanding that challenges are opportunities for growth and resilience, you can develop effective strategies to navigate through difficult times and emerge stronger and more empowered.

Stress Management

Higher education can be demanding, leading to stress and anxiety among students. Managing stress is essential for students to maintain their well-being and navigate the challenges of higher education. Let's look at some very practical tips and techniques to effectively manage stress and anxiety:

a. **Practice Mindfulness:** Take a few moments each day to cultivate mindfulness. Engage in activities such as deep breathing exercises, meditation, or yoga. By focusing on the present moment and nurturing a sense of awareness, you can better manage stress triggers and find inner calm amidst the busyness of student life.

b. **Engage in Physical Activity:** Incorporate regular exercise into your routine. Whether it's going for a jog, hitting the gym, or participating in a dance class, physical activity releases endorphins and helps alleviate stress. Find activities that you enjoy and make them a part of your self-care regimen.

c. **Ask for Help:** Remember, you don't have to face stress alone. Reach out to counsellors, therapists, or support groups available on your campus. These professionals are trained to provide guidance and support during challenging times. Don't hesitate to seek their assistance whenever you feel overwhelmed or in need of someone to talk to.

d. **Self-Care:** Make self-care a priority. Schedule regular breaks, get enough sleep, and engage in activities that bring you joy and relaxation. It's crucial to take care of your physical, mental, and emotional well-being to manage stress effectively.

e. **Journalling:** Consider keeping a journal as a means of self-expression. Write down your thoughts, emotions, and reflections. Journalling can provide a therapeutic outlet for stress and help you gain clarity and perspective. It's a valuable tool for self-reflection, gratitude, and problem-solving.

f. **Engage in Hobbies and Recreation:** Dedicate time to activities you enjoy and that help you unwind. Engaging in hobbies, whether it's painting, playing a musical instrument, or cooking, can provide a much-needed break from academic pressures. These activities promote relaxation, creativity, and overall well-being.

HANDLING ACADEMIC PRESSURES

Higher education often comes with a rigorous academic workload and high expectations. In this section, we will learn simple strategies for managing academic pressures, including effective time management, setting realistic goals, and seeking academic assistance when needed.

It highlights the importance of breaking tasks into smaller, manageable chunks, maintaining a study schedule, and utilising resources such as tutoring services or study groups.

a. **Effective Time Management:** Managing your time efficiently is crucial for handling academic pressures. Create a schedule that outlines your study time, assignments, and other commitments. Prioritise tasks based on urgency and importance. Break down larger tasks into smaller, manageable chunks to make them more approachable. Utilise time management techniques such as the Pomodoro Technique, where you work for a set period and then take short breaks. By managing your time effectively, you'll feel more in control and better equipped to handle your academic workload.

b. Establishing a consistent study schedule helps create a structured routine and promotes productivity. Determine the times of day when you are most alert and focused, and allocate those periods for studying. Find a study environment that works best for you, whether it's a quiet library or a comfortable corner in your hostel room. Minimise distractions by turning off notifications on your electronic devices and practising disciplined study habits.

c. **Seek Academic Assistance:** Don't hesitate to seek academic assistance when needed. If you're struggling with a particular subject or concept, reach out to your professors, teaching assistants, or academic support centres. Take advantage of tutoring services or study groups to gain a better understanding of the material. Collaborating with peers can provide a fresh perspective and make studying more engaging and enjoyable.

d. **Utilise Resources:** Take advantage of the resources available to you. Many universities offer academic support services, such as writing centres, math labs, or subject-specific workshops. These resources can provide additional guidance and support in challenging areas. Seek out online platforms, educational websites, or instructional videos that can supplement your learning and offer alternative explanations of complex topics.

BALANCING PERSONAL AND ACADEMIC LIFE

As a student, you often find yourself juggling various personal commitments, a vibrant social life, and the demands of your academic responsibilities. Achieving a healthy balance between these different aspects can be a significant challenge. It requires self-discipline, and the ability to prioritise tasks. Here's a closer look at how you can navigate this balancing act:

a. **Prioritise Tasks:** Start by identifying your priorities and allocating time accordingly. Determine which tasks are urgent, important, or can be postponed. Focus on completing high-priority tasks first and break larger tasks into smaller, manageable steps. By prioritising your tasks, you can ensure that you're dedicating time to the most critical responsibilities while maintaining a balance with personal commitments.

b. **Set Boundaries:** Establish clear boundaries between your academic and personal life. Designate specific times for studying and coursework, and communicate these boundaries to your friends, family, and peers. Let them know when you're not available or need uninterrupted time for academic commitments. By setting boundaries, you can protect your personal time and create a healthy balance between your academic and social life.

c. **Establish Realistic Expectations:** Be realistic in your expectations of what you can achieve academically and personally. Avoid putting excessive pressure on yourself to excel in every aspect of your life simultaneously. Set realistic goals and prioritise self-care. Recognise that balance does not mean perfection but rather finding harmony between different areas of your life. Be kind to yourself and celebrate your achievements, no matter how small they may seem.

d. **Ask for help and Delegate:** Don't hesitate to seek support and delegate tasks when necessary. Reach out to family, friends, or classmates for assistance when you need it. Collaborate on group projects, study together, or divide responsibilities to ease the workload. Asking for help is not a sign of weakness but a practical way to manage your time and create balance.

CASE STUDY: GAUTAM'S JOURNEY TO BALANCING PERSONAL AND ACADEMIC LIFE

Gautam, a final-year BTech student, had always been ambitious and driven to excel in his academics. However, as he approached his final year, the pressure of placements and projects started taking a toll on him. Struggling to balance his personal life with the academic demands, Gautam found himself overwhelmed and on the verge of jeopardising his chances of landing a great job. This case study follows Gautam's journey as he recognised the issue, took effective steps to contain the situation, and ultimately achieved success in his final exams and secured a high-paying job.

Challenge 1: Overwhelming Burden of Placements and Projects:

Gautam's final year brought along a heavy workload, including numerous project submissions and the stress of campus placements. He found himself constantly engrossed in academic commitments, neglecting his personal life and well-being.

Solution: Realising the need for balance, Gautam took proactive steps to manage his workload more effectively. He created a detailed study schedule that allowed him to allocate time for both academic tasks and personal activities. Gautam prioritised his projects based on deadlines and the effort required for each one. He sought guidance from professors and seniors to streamline his project work, focusing on the most critical aspects. By planning and breaking down his tasks into manageable chunks, Gautam was able to regain control over his academic commitments.

Challenge 2: Regaining Academic Focus and Improving Grades:

With his grades slipping, Gautam realised the urgent need to regain his academic focus and perform well in his final exams. He knew that strong academic performance was crucial for securing a high-paying job.

Solution: Gautam adopted effective study strategies and sought academic guidance from professors and tutors. He reviewed his study techniques and explored new approaches such as active learning, mnemonic devices, and self-quizzing. Gautam also formed study groups with classmates, allowing them to collaborate, share knowledge, and hold each other accountable. He regularly attended extra coaching classes and sought clarification on challenging topics. By implementing these strategies, Gautam improved his understanding of the subjects, regained his academic focus, and performed exceptionally well in his final exams.

Challenge 3: Securing a High-Paying Job:

As Gautam's final year progressed, he faced the additional challenge of impressing recruiters during placement interviews. His initial struggles had affected his confidence, and he feared that he would not land a desirable job opportunity.

Solution: Gautam actively worked on boosting his confidence and interview skills. He participated in mock interview sessions conducted by the college's placement cell and sought feedback from recruiters. Gautam researched the companies he was interested in and prepared well for specific job roles and technical interviews. He also enhanced his resume by highlighting his project accomplishments and relevant skills. Through persistence and dedication, Gautam's hard work paid off, and he secured a high-paying job with a renowned company.

Gautam's journey exemplifies the challenges faced by many students in balancing personal and academic life. By recognising the issue and taking proactive steps to regain control, Gautam successfully managed the overwhelming academic demands. Through effective time management and adopting focused study strategies, Gautam improved his academic performance and regained his confidence.

CHAPTER 12

CRAFTING POWERFUL RESUMES FOR ACADEMIC AND PROFESSIONAL SUCCESS

A well-crafted resume is crucial in presenting your skills, qualifications, and accomplishments to potential employers, scholarship committees, or academic institutions. Whether you are a student preparing for internships or a working professional seeking career advancement, understanding the key components and strategies for creating impactful resumes is essential. In this chapter, we will explore the art of writing powerful resumes that effectively highlight the academic achievements and professional experiences.

UNDERSTANDING THE PURPOSE OF A RESUME

A powerful resume is highly significant in capturing the attention of potential employers or admissions committees. A resume acts as a powerful marketing tool, enabling you to showcase your unique set of skills, experiences, and accomplishments that make you a standout candidate.

The primary purpose of a resume is to provide a concise and compelling snapshot of your qualifications and achievements. It serves as a gateway to grab the attention of recruiters and create a positive first impression. In a competitive job market or academic admissions process, a well-crafted resume can make all the difference in setting you apart from other applicants.

A resume is a strategic document that highlights your most relevant and impactful achievements. It is crucial to tailor your resume for each opportunity, focusing on the skills and experiences that align with the specific requirements of the job or academic programme you are applying to. By doing so, you demonstrate your attention to detail and genuine interest in the position or programme.

When crafting your resume, keep in mind the limited time that recruiters or admissions committees have to review each application. Your resume needs to make an immediate and positive impression. It should be clear, concise, and well-organised, with the information presented in a format that is easy to navigate and comprehend. Utilise bullet points, headings, and appropriate formatting techniques to enhance readability and highlight key information.

Remember, a resume is not meant to be an exhaustive account of your entire academic and professional history. It is a strategic selection of your most relevant experiences, skills, and achievements that showcase your potential to excel in a specific role or academic programme. Therefore, it is important to carefully choose the information you include, focusing on the most impactful and pertinent details.

ACADEMIC RESUMES

Academic resumes are commonly used by students, researchers, and educators. They highlight academic achievements, research projects, publications, presentations, and relevant coursework. Here are key points to consider when crafting an academic resume:

1. **Organise your resume with clear sections:** Start with your education section, listing your degrees, majors, and the institution you attended. Follow this with sections such as research experience, publications, honours, and extracurricular activities. This helps the reader quickly navigate through your resume and find the information they are looking for.

2. **Emphasise academic achievements:** Highlight any scholarships, awards, or honours you have received throughout

your academic journey. This showcases your academic excellence and distinguishes you from other candidates.

3. **Include research experience:** If you have been involved in research projects, provide a brief description of the projects, the methodologies used, and the outcomes achieved. This demonstrates your ability to engage in scholarly work and contribute to the advancement of knowledge in your field.

4. **Highlight relevant coursework and academic projects:** Mention any coursework or academic projects that are directly related to the position or academic programme you are applying for. This shows your knowledge and expertise in specific areas and indicates your readiness to tackle advanced academic challenges.

5. **Mention leadership roles and participation in conferences:** If you have held leadership positions in student organisations or have participated in conferences or symposiums, include these experiences. They demonstrate your ability to take on responsibilities and engage with the academic community.

PROFESSIONAL RESUMES

Professional resumes are designed for individuals with work experience seeking job opportunities or career advancement. Here are essential tips for creating a powerful professional resume:

Creating a powerful professional resume is crucial for individuals with work experience who are seeking job opportunities or career advancement. Here are some essential tips to help you craft an impactful professional resume:

1. **Start with a strong professional summary or objective statement:** This section should grab the reader's attention and provide a concise overview of your skills, experience, and career goals. Tailor it to match the specific job or industry you are targeting.

2. **Include a clear and concise work experience section:** List your previous job titles, company names, employment dates, and key responsibilities. Focus on showcasing your achievements and the impact you made in your previous roles. Use action verbs and quantitative data to demonstrate your accomplishments.

3. **Highlight your accomplishments and quantifiable achievements:** Employers value measurable results, so include specific achievements that showcase your skills and contributions. For example, mention how you exceeded sales targets, implemented cost-saving initiatives, or completed projects on time and within budget.

4. **Incorporate relevant skills:** Include a dedicated skills section that highlights both hard and soft skills relevant to the job you are applying for. Tailor your skills to match the requirements listed in the job description, and provide examples of how you have applied these skills in previous roles.

5. **Include relevant certifications, professional development courses, and industry affiliations:** If you have obtained any certifications, completed professional development courses, or are a member of relevant industry organisations, mention them in this section. This demonstrates your commitment to continuous learning and professional growth.

6. **Provide a section for education:** Mention your degree(s), the university name, graduation year, and any academic distinctions or honours. If you have significant work experience, this section can be placed below the work experience section.

FORMATTING AND DESIGN

Pay attention to the formatting and design of your resume to ensure it is visually appealing and easy to read. Here are some tips:

- Use clear headings, subheadings, and bullet points to organise information.

- Choose a professional font and font size that is easy to read.

- Maintain consistency in formatting, such as using the same bullet point style and indentation throughout the document.

- Use appropriate spacing and margins to create a clean and organised layout.

Remember to tailor your resume for each job application, highlighting the most relevant skills and experiences. A well-crafted professional resume can make a strong impression on employers and increase your chances of securing job interviews and career opportunities.

TAILORING YOUR RESUME

Tailoring your resume is a crucial step in the application process, as it allows you to showcase your most relevant qualifications and experiences to match the specific requirements of each opportunity. Here are some tips to help you tailor your resume effectively:

- **Review the job description or scholarship requirements:** Carefully read and understand the job description or scholarship requirements to identify the key skills, qualifications, and experiences sought by the employer or scholarship committee.

- **Identify the most relevant qualifications:** Match your own skills, experiences, and achievements with the requirements outlined in the job description or scholarship criteria. Highlight the qualifications that directly align with the needs of the position or scholarship.

- **Customise your professional summary or objective statement:** Tailor your professional summary or objective statement to reflect your alignment with the specific job or scholarship. Use keywords and phrases from the description to demonstrate your suitability and interest.

- **Modify your work experience section:** Adjust the content of your work experience section to emphasise the responsibilities, achievements, and skills that are most relevant to the position or scholarship. Include specific examples and measurable outcomes that demonstrate your competence in those areas.

- **Highlight relevant coursework, projects, and skills:** If you are a student or recent graduate, consider including relevant coursework, academic projects, and skills that directly relate to the position or scholarship. This demonstrates your academic preparation and ability to apply your knowledge to real-world situations.

- **Rearrange sections and prioritise information:** Reorder the sections of your resume to prioritise the most relevant information. If your education or relevant coursework is more applicable to the opportunity, move it above the work experience section.

- **Customise your skills section:** Tailor your skills section to highlight the skills that are most sought after in the job or scholarship. Use keywords from the description and provide specific examples of how you have demonstrated those skills.

- **Quantify your achievements:** Whenever possible, quantify your achievements and provide measurable results to showcase the impact you have made in your previous experiences. This helps to demonstrate your effectiveness and the value you can bring to the role or organisation.

The goal of tailoring your resume is to demonstrate your fit for the specific opportunity and make it easy for the reader to see why you are a strong candidate. Take the time to customise your resume for each application, as it can significantly increase your chances of success.

PROOFREADING AND EDITING

Proofreading and editing are crucial steps to ensure your resume is polished and error-free. Here are some tips to help you in this process:

- **Review for grammar and spelling errors:** Carefully read through your resume to catch any grammatical errors, typos, or spelling mistakes. Use spelling and grammar check tools, but also manually review the content to ensure accuracy.

- **Check for formatting consistency:** Ensure that the formatting, font, and spacing are consistent throughout your resume. Pay attention to bullet points, indentation, and alignment. Make sure your headings and subheadings are clear and consistent.

- **Seek feedback from others:** Share your resume with mentors, professors, or career counsellors and ask for their feedback. They can provide valuable insights and suggestions for improvement, as well as identify any areas that may need clarification or further development.

- **Have a final review:** Before submitting your resume, conduct a final review to ensure that all changes have been implemented correctly and that your resume is error-free. Take the time to carefully read through your entire resume to make sure it flows well and effectively communicates your qualifications.

Example:

Here's an example of a well-structured and professionally designed resume:

[Your Name]

[Contact Information: Phone Number, Email Address, LinkedIn Profile]

Objective:

A highly motivated and detail-oriented professional seeking a challenging role in [desired field] to utilise [relevant skills] and contribute to the success of [target organisation]. Committed to delivering exceptional results and continuously expanding knowledge in [specific area].

Education:

Bachelor of Science in [Major], [University Name], [Graduation Year]

Relevant coursework: [Course 1], [Course 2], [Course 3]

Academic achievements: [Honours, Awards, Scholarships]

Work Experience:

[Job Title], [Company/Organisation], [Employment Dates]

- Conducted market research and analysis to identify new business opportunities
- Developed and implemented marketing strategies that increased customer engagement by 20%
- Collaborated with cross-functional teams to execute successful product launches
- Managed client relationships and consistently exceeded customer satisfaction targets

Skills:

- Proficient in [Software/Tools]
- Strong analytical and problem-solving abilities
- Excellent communication and interpersonal skills
- Project management and multitasking
- Attention to detail and ability to meet deadlines

Professional Certifications:

[Certification 1], [Certifying Organisation], [Year]

[Certification 2], [Certifying Organisation], [Year]

Leadership and Extracurricular Activities:

President, [Student Organisation], [Year] - Led a team of 15 members in organising various events and initiatives

Volunteer, [Non-profit Organisation], [Year] - Contributed to community service projects and fundraisers

References:

Available upon request

This is just an example, and you should customise the content and format based on your own experiences, skills, and industry requirements. Pay attention to the organisation and clarity of information, use bullet points to highlight accomplishments, and ensure that your resume is error-free and visually appealing.

VIDEO RESUMES

In recent years, video resumes have gained popularity as an alternative way to showcase your skills and qualifications. Here are some tips for creating an effective video resume:

1. **Plan your content:** Before recording your video, plan what you want to include. Think about the key points you want to highlight, such as your skills, experiences, and achievements. Consider the job or industry you're targeting and tailor your content accordingly.

2. **Keep it concise:** Video resumes should be brief and to the point. Aim for 1-2 minutes to ensure that the viewer remains engaged. Focus on your most relevant qualifications and experiences, and avoid rambling or excessive details.

3. **Introduce yourself:** Begin your video by introducing yourself and providing a brief overview of your background and qualifications. Clearly state your name, educational background, and any notable achievements or experiences.

4. **Showcase your skills and experiences:** Use the video to highlight your key skills, experiences, and accomplishments. Provide specific examples of how you have applied your skills in previous roles or projects. Use visuals, such as slides

or images, to enhance your presentation and make it more engaging.

5. **Be professional and enthusiastic:** Treat your video resume as a professional presentation. Dress appropriately, maintain good posture, and speak clearly and confidently. Show enthusiasm for the role or industry you are targeting to convey your passion and commitment.

6. **Pay attention to the background and lighting:** Choose a clean and professional-looking background for your video. Ensure that the lighting is sufficient and that there are no distractions or clutter in the frame. Good lighting and a clear background will help the viewer focus on your message.

7. **Practice and rehearse:** Before recording your video resume, practice what you want to say and how you want to say it. Rehearse your presentation to ensure a smooth delivery. Consider recording yourself multiple times to get comfortable in front of the camera and improve your performance.

8. **Edit and review:** Once you have recorded your video, edit it to remove any unnecessary footage or mistakes. Review the final video to ensure that it flows well and effectively communicates your qualifications. Seek feedback from trusted individuals to get an outside perspective and make any necessary improvements.

9. **Share appropriately:** When sharing your video resume, consider the platform or context in which it will be viewed. Some employers may prefer a link to your video resume, while others may request a specific file format. Follow the instructions provided by the employer or platform to ensure that your video is easily accessible.

Remember, video resumes should complement your traditional resume and not replace it. Consider using a video resume when it aligns with the industry or job you are applying for and when it allows you to showcase your personality and communication skills effectively.

Using Online Resume Builder

Using an online resume template can be a convenient and efficient way to create a professional-looking resume. Here are some tips for using online templates effectively:

- **Choose a reputable platform:** There are several online platforms that offer resume templates. Ensure that you choose a reputable and reliable platform that provides high-quality templates. I use Canva and Novoresume.com.

- **Select a template that suits your needs:** Browse through the available templates and select one that aligns with your industry, career level, and personal preferences. Consider the layout, design elements, and sections included in the template.

- **Customise the template:** Once you have selected a template, customise it to fit your specific qualifications and experiences. Replace the placeholder text with your own information, including your name, contact details, work experience, education, and skills. Adjust the sections, fonts, and colours as needed.

- **Focus on content:** While the template provides a professional layout, the content you include is essential. Tailor the content to highlight your relevant qualifications and achievements. Be concise, use strong action verbs, and quantify your accomplishments when possible.

- **Review and proofread:** After customising the template, review your resume to ensure that it is error-free and well-organised. Proofread the content for any spelling or grammatical errors. Consider seeking feedback from a trusted friend, mentor, or career coach to ensure that your resume is clear and effective.

- **Save in an appropriate format:** When saving your resume, consider the preferred format of the recipient or the application requirements. PDF is often the preferred format as it preserves the formatting and ensures that your resume appears as intended when opened on different devices.

- **Regularly update your resume:** As you gain new experiences, skills, or achievements, remember to update your resume accordingly. Keep your resume up-to-date to reflect your most recent qualifications and ensure that it remains relevant to potential employers.

While online resume templates can provide a good starting point, it's important to customise the template to make it unique and tailored to your specific needs. Avoid using generic or overly common templates that may not help you stand out from other applicants. Ultimately, your resume should effectively communicate your qualifications and make a positive impression on employers.

Crafting powerful resumes is a critical skill for academic and professional success. A well-written resume can open doors to new opportunities and help you stand out among other candidates. By following the guidelines and strategies outlined in this chapter, you can create compelling resumes that effectively showcase your qualifications, experiences, and achievements, increasing your chances of achieving your academic and career goals.

CHAPTER 13

MASTERING INTERVIEW PREPARATION

Interviews can be nerve-wracking, especially if it's your first time. Before we delve into cracking the interview, let's gain insight into what's inside an interviewer's mind. Having been an interviewer myself and having interviewed thousands of young individuals, I can confidently say that an interviewer's job is not to reject candidates but to create opportunities for them to shine. So, go into the interview with confidence, knowing that they are eager to see you succeed.

A PEEK INSIDE THE RECRUITER'S MIND

Here are some expectations that recruiters or interviewers have during the interview, along with how you can consider them while preparing:

- **Confidence:** One of the most crucial expectations is your confidence. Display self-assurance in your abilities and qualifications. Confidence portrays your belief in yourself and your potential contributions to the organisation.

- **Communication Skills:** While exceptional English proficiency isn't mandatory, having decent communication and articulation skills is essential. Be clear and concise in your responses, and ensure that you express your thoughts effectively.

- **Subject Knowledge:** Demonstrate a strong understanding of your subject matter. Be prepared to discuss relevant concepts, theories, and experiences related to the role you are applying for.

- **Past Experiences:** Highlight any past experiences that are relevant to the job. This could include internships, volunteer work, or projects that showcase your skills and accomplishments.

- **Authenticity and Character:** Be true to yourself during the interview. Don't try to portray a version of yourself that isn't genuine. Interviewers appreciate candidates who are authentic and showcase their true character.

- **Honesty:** If you encounter a question you don't know the answer to, it's okay to say, "I don't know." Honesty is appreciated, and interviewers understand that not every candidate will have all the answers.

- **Humility:** Sometimes, extra-smart candidates lose out to humble candidates who are to themselves. Emphasise your character and attitude throughout the interview.

Remember, skills can be taught and developed over time, but character is fundamental and valued. So, focus on presenting yourself genuinely, displaying confidence, and communicating effectively. With the right approach and preparation, you can make a positive impression and increase your chances of success in the interview process.

PRACTICAL TIPS AND STRATEGIES TO MAXIMISE SUCCESS IN A JOB INTERVIEW

Preparing for job interviews is a crucial step in the job search process. In the following section, I have shared guidance on how to effectively prepare for job interviews, practical tips, techniques, and strategies to maximise success.

1. **Researching the Company:**

   Researching the company is a vital step in preparing for a job interview. It helps to gather valuable information that can help you make a positive impression on the interviewer and tailor your responses to align with the company's goals and culture. Here are some tips and strategies for effective company research:

a. **Explore the Company's Website:**

   Start by visiting the company's official website. Look for sections such as "About Us", "Mission and Values", and "Company Culture". These sections provide insights into the company's history, core values, and overall mission. Take note of any unique aspects or initiatives that align with your own values and interests.

b. **Review Recent News and Press Releases:**

   Check for recent news articles, press releases, or blog posts related to the company. This will help you stay updated on the latest developments, product launches, collaborations, or achievements. Understanding the company's recent successes or challenges can provide valuable talking points during the interview.

c. **Explore Social Media Channels:**

   Social media platforms can offer additional insights into the company's culture, brand identity, and engagement with its audience. Follow the company on platforms such as LinkedIn, Twitter, Facebook, or Instagram. Pay attention to the content they share, their interactions with customers or followers, and any relevant industry trends or discussions they participate in.

d. **Investigate the Company's Competitors:**

   Researching the company's competitors can provide valuable context and help you understand its position in the industry. Explore the competitors' websites, their strengths and weaknesses, and how the company differentiates itself. This knowledge can be useful when discussing the company's competitive advantage or when addressing questions related to industry trends during the interview.

e. **Utilise Professional Networking Platforms:**

Professional networking platforms like LinkedIn can be excellent resources for gathering information about the company. Look for profiles of current or former employees to gain insights into their experiences and perspectives. Connecting with employees who work or have worked at the company can provide valuable insider insights and potentially open doors for informational interviews.

f. **Seek Information from Current or Former Employees:**

If you have contacts who work or have worked at the company, reach out to them for a conversation. They can provide valuable insights into the company's culture, work environment, and interview process. Prepare thoughtful questions to gather meaningful information and be respectful of their time.

g. **Carefully read the Job Description:**

Thoroughly review the job description to understand the specific requirements and responsibilities of the role you are interviewing for. Pay attention to the keywords, skills, and qualifications mentioned. This will help you tailor your responses during the interview to highlight your relevant experiences and abilities.

By conducting thorough research, you demonstrate your genuine interest in the company and the role. It allows you to ask thoughtful questions during the interview and enables you to connect your skills and experiences with the company's goals and values. Incorporate the information you gather into your interview preparation to confidently showcase your knowledge and passion for the company.

Remember, effective company research goes beyond surface-level information. It involves digging deeper to understand the company's mission, values, products or services, target market, recent developments, and industry position. By demonstrating a comprehensive understanding of the company, you can differentiate yourself from other candidates and leave a lasting impression on the interviewer.

2. **Practising Common Interview Questions:**

Practising common interview questions is a valuable strategy for preparing yourself to confidently and effectively communicate during a job interview. By anticipating and rehearsing potential questions, you can refine your responses and present yourself in the best possible light. Here are some practical tips for practising common interview questions:

a. **Research Common Interview Questions:**

Start by researching common interview questions that are often asked in your industry or for the specific type of job you are applying for. Online resources, career websites, and interview preparation guides can provide lists of commonly asked questions. Compile a comprehensive list of questions that you can use as a reference during your practice sessions.

b. **Understand the Intent Behind the Questions:**

While practising, it's important to understand the purpose behind each question. Consider what the interviewer is trying to assess through each question. For example, questions about your strengths are designed to evaluate your self-awareness and ability to align your strengths with the requirements of the job. By understanding the intent behind the questions, you can tailor your responses to address the underlying criteria.

c.   **Prepare Structured Responses:**

Once you have a list of common interview questions, take the time to prepare well-structured responses. Start by outlining the main points you want to cover in your answer. Be concise and ensure that your response directly addresses the question asked. Use the STAR method (Situation, Task, Action, Result) to structure your responses to behavioural questions, providing specific examples of past experiences or achievements.

d.   **Practice Out Loud:**

Practice your responses out loud to get comfortable articulating your thoughts verbally. This will help you develop fluency, clarity, and confidence in your delivery. Focus on speaking clearly and maintaining a positive and professional tone. You can practice alone or with a friend or family member who can provide feedback and help simulate an interview setting.

e.   **Time Your Responses:**

During an interview, time is limited, and it's important to deliver concise and focused responses. Time yourself when practising your answers to ensure that you stay within a reasonable timeframe. Aim for responses that are clear, comprehensive, and around one to two minutes in length. Being mindful of time will help you maintain a concise and engaging communication style.

f.   **Seek Feedback:**

Consider seeking feedback from someone you trust, such as a mentor, career coach, or even a trusted friend or family member. They can provide valuable insights on the clarity and effectiveness of your responses, as well as offer suggestions for improvement. Pay attention to their feedback and make necessary adjustments to enhance the impact of your answers.

g. **Record Yourself:**

Another effective technique is to record yourself practising your responses. Use a smartphone or a recording device to capture your practice sessions. This allows you to review your performance, assess your body language, and identify areas where you can improve. Be attentive to your tone, facial expressions, and overall presentation.

The goal of practising common interview questions is not to memorise scripted answers. Instead, it is to develop a clear understanding of your qualifications, experiences, and how you can effectively communicate them to the interviewer.

3. **Showcasing Skills and Experiences:**

Showcasing skills and experiences effectively during a job interview can significantly impact how you are perceived by the interviewer. It is essential to carefully select and present relevant examples that highlight your qualifications, achievements, and strengths. Here are some tips to help you showcase your skills and experiences effectively:

a. **Understand the Job Requirements:**

Before the interview, thoroughly review the job description and identify the key skills and qualifications that are required for the role. Take note of the specific skills and experiences that are mentioned and think about how your own experiences align with them. This will help you tailor your responses and focus on showcasing the most relevant skills during the interview.

b. **Prepare Examples:**

Prepare a list of specific examples from your past experiences that demonstrate your skills and abilities. These examples should highlight achievements, problem-solving skills, teamwork, leadership, or any other relevant competencies. Select examples that are recent, significant, and demonstrate your ability to overcome challenges or achieve results.

c. **Use the STAR Method:**

When sharing examples during the interview, use the STAR method (Situation, Task, Action, Result) to structure your responses. Start by briefly explaining the situation or context in which the example occurred. Then, describe the specific task or challenge you faced. Next, explain the actions you took to address the situation, highlighting the skills and qualities you utilised. Finally, share the results or outcomes of your actions, emphasising any positive impacts or achievements.

d. **Quantify Achievements:**

Whenever possible, quantify your achievements to provide tangible evidence of your capabilities. For example, instead of saying you improved a process, mention the percentage increase in efficiency that resulted from your efforts. Quantifying your achievements adds credibility to your claims and helps the interviewer understand the value you can bring to the organisation.

e. **Tailor Examples to the Job Requirements:**

As you share your examples, make sure to highlight how your skills and experiences directly relate to the job requirements. Emphasise how your past experiences have prepared you for the challenges and responsibilities of the role. This demonstrates your ability to transfer your skills and shows the interviewer that you are a good fit for the position.

f. **Practice Active Listening:**

During the interview, actively listen to the questions and concerns raised by the interviewer. This allows you to respond in a way that addresses their specific needs and showcases your relevant skills and experiences. If you notice any specific skills or experiences being emphasised in their questions, try to incorporate those into your responses to further highlight your qualifications.

g. **Be Enthusiastic and Confident:**

As you share your examples, be enthusiastic and confident in your delivery. Show genuine passion for your experiences and accomplishments. Maintain eye contact, speak clearly and concisely, and use positive body language. Your enthusiasm and confidence will help the interviewer connect with your stories and leave a lasting impression.

Remember, the goal of showcasing your skills and experiences is to demonstrate your qualifications and convince the interviewer of your capabilities. By carefully selecting relevant examples, using the STAR method, quantifying achievements, and tailoring your responses to the job requirements, you can effectively showcase your skills and experiences during a job interview.

4. **Demonstrating Adaptability and Problem-solving Skills:**

Employers value candidates who can adapt to new situations and solve problems effectively. During the interview, candidates should be prepared to discuss scenarios where they faced challenges, found innovative solutions, and demonstrated resilience. This showcases their ability to think critically, handle pressure, and contribute positively to the organisation. Here are some tips on how to effectively demonstrate these skills during an interview:

a. **Share Relevant Examples:**

Prepare examples from your past experiences where you faced challenges or encountered situations that required adaptability and problem-solving skills. These examples can come from academic projects, internships, part-time jobs, or extracurricular activities. Select examples that highlight your ability to think on your feet, remain calm under pressure, and come up with creative solutions.

b. **Describe the Challenge:**

When discussing your examples, start by clearly describing the challenge or problem you encountered. Explain the context, the specific obstacles you faced, and the potential implications of not finding a solution. This helps the interviewer understand the significance of the situation and the level of complexity involved.

c. **Outline Your Approach:**

Next, explain the approach you took to address the challenge. Describe the steps you followed to analyse the problem, gather relevant information, and consider different perspectives. Highlight your critical thinking skills and your ability to break down complex problems into manageable components.

d. **Emphasise Adaptability:**

During the interview, emphasise how you adapted your approach to address the challenge. Discuss any changes you made to your original plan based on new information or unexpected circumstances. This demonstrates your flexibility and willingness to adjust your strategies when necessary.

e. **Highlight Problem-solving Techniques:**

Describe the problem-solving techniques or methodologies you used to reach a solution. This could include brainstorming, root cause analysis, SWOT analysis, or other problem-solving frameworks. Explain how you applied these techniques and the results they helped you achieve.

f.   **Discuss Results and Impact:**

Finally, share the outcomes of your problem-solving efforts and the impact they had. Highlight any positive results, such as improved efficiency, cost savings, increased customer satisfaction, or successful project completion. Quantify the impact whenever possible to provide concrete evidence of your problem-solving abilities.

g.   **Reflect on Lessons Learned:**

After discussing the results, reflect on the lessons you learned from the experience. Discuss how this particular challenge enhanced your adaptability and problem-solving skills, and how you have applied these skills in subsequent situations. This demonstrates your ability to learn from past experiences and continuously improve.

h.   **Connect to the Role:**

Throughout your discussion, make connections between your examples and the requirements of the role you are applying for. Show how your adaptability and problem-solving skills align with the job responsibilities and how they can contribute to the organisation's success. This helps the interviewer envision you as a valuable asset to their team.

Be clear, concise, and confident when sharing your examples. Use the STAR method as discussed above (Situation, Task, Action, Result) to structure your responses and provide a clear framework for your examples. Remember that by effectively showcasing your adaptability and problem-solving skills, you can leave a lasting impression on the interviewer and increase your chances of securing the job.

Case Study: Ajay's First Interview Success

Ajay, a recent graduate, was excited and nervous as he prepared for his first job interview. He had been invited to interview for a junior marketing role at a well-known company. Determined to make a positive impression, Ajay took several steps to prepare for the interview.

First, Ajay conducted thorough research on the company. He explored their website, read their annual reports, and familiarised himself with their products and services. He also researched the industry trends and market positioning of the company to gain a broader understanding of its competitive landscape. Ajay's research allowed him to showcase his knowledge and enthusiasm about the company during the interview.

Next, Ajay prepared responses to common interview questions. He practised answering questions about his background, strengths and weaknesses, and why he was interested in the marketing field. Ajay made sure his answers were concise and clear and highlighted relevant experiences from his coursework, internships, and extracurricular activities. He also prepared specific examples of his problem-solving abilities, adaptability, and teamwork skills to showcase during the interview.

To further enhance his preparation, Ajay conducted a mock interview with a friend. They simulated a real interview scenario, with the friend asking Ajay a variety of interview questions. This practice helped Ajay refine his responses, gain confidence in his communication skills, and improve his overall interview performance.

On the day of the interview, Ajay dressed professionally and arrived early at the company's office. He greeted the receptionist with a warm smile and maintained a positive attitude throughout the entire process. During the interview, Ajay actively listened to the interviewer's questions, carefully considered his responses, and provided specific examples to support his answers.

Ajay also asked thoughtful questions about the company's marketing strategies, opportunities for growth, and team dynamic. This demonstrated his genuine interest in the role and his enthusiasm for learning more about the company's objectives and vision.

Throughout the interview, Ajay showcased his passion for marketing and his ability to think critically and creatively. He confidently discussed his experiences working on marketing campaigns during his internships, highlighting the results achieved and the strategies he employed. Ajay's well-prepared responses, combined with his positive attitude and genuine enthusiasm, left a strong impression on the interviewer.

Days later, Ajay received the exciting news that he had been offered the job. The interviewer praised his knowledge, enthusiasm, and ability to effectively communicate his qualifications and fit for the role. Ajay's dedication to preparation and his ability to showcase his skills and passion during the interview set him apart from other candidates and ultimately led to his success.

This case study demonstrates the importance of thorough preparation, research, and confident communication in securing a job offer. By investing time and effort in understanding the company, preparing responses to interview questions, and practising his interview skills, Ajay was able to convince the interviewer of his qualifications and land his first job in the marketing field.

Every interview is an opportunity to showcase your abilities and make a positive impression. By following Ajay's example and preparing well, you too can increase your chances of interview success and secure your desired job.

Note: This case study is fictional and created for illustrative purposes.

CREATIVE STRATEGIES FOR ANSWERING BASIC QUESTIONS WITH IMPACT

Let's now explore effective strategies for answering basic interview questions in a creative and impactful manner, maximising your chances of success. Rather than copying answers verbatim, the goal is to draw inspiration and develop unique responses that highlight your strengths and experiences.

i. **"Tell me something about yourself."**

Instead of reciting your resume, use this opportunity to captivate the interviewer by sharing a compelling story that showcases your passion, values, and relevant experiences. Craft a narrative that emphasises key milestones in your career, highlighting your growth, achievements, and the skills you have developed along the way.

ii. **"Why are you interested in this position?"**

Go beyond surface-level motivations and demonstrate your deep understanding of the company and its values. Discuss how your own aspirations and goals align with the organisation's mission and how your unique skill set can contribute to its success. Incorporate specific details about the company's recent accomplishments or initiatives to show your genuine interest.

iii. **"What are your strengths?"**

Rather than providing a generic list of strengths, illustrate each strength with a concise anecdote or example that demonstrates how you have effectively utilised it in a professional setting. Emphasise the impact of your strengths by highlighting tangible results or successful outcomes that you have achieved.

iv. **"What is your greatest weakness?"**

Rather than dwelling on weaknesses, focus on areas where you have recognised opportunities for growth and improvement. Discuss how you have actively sought to develop these areas through self-directed learning, seeking feedback, or taking on challenging projects. Highlight your commitment to personal development and showcase how you have turned weaknesses into strengths.

v. **"Describe a challenging situation and how you resolved it."**

Select a relevant and significant challenge you faced in a professional setting, clearly outlining the problem, the actions you took, and the positive outcomes that resulted. Highlight your problem-solving skills, resilience, and ability to collaborate with others. Focus on your adaptability and creative thinking to showcase your ability to navigate complex situations.

vi.   **"How do you handle working in a team?"**

Instead of simply stating that you work well in teams, provide a specific example that demonstrates your collaborative abilities. Discuss a project or situation where you effectively communicated, leveraged the strengths of team members, and contributed to achieving a common goal. Highlight your ability to foster a positive team dynamic and create synergy.

vii.   **"Tell me about a time you demonstrated leadership."**

Share a specific leadership experience where you took initiative, influenced others, and achieved positive outcomes. Describe the actions you took, the challenges you faced, and the impact you made. Highlight your ability to inspire, motivate, and empower others, and how you effectively navigated through obstacles to drive success.

The key is to use these ideas as a springboard to craft your own responses. Tailor your answers to your unique experiences, skills, and specific job requirements. Be authentic, confident, and focus on showcasing your abilities in a way that resonates with the interviewer.

Ajay Khanna's 3P Model for Sure shot Success

Prepare	Present	Perform
• Research: • Self-Assessment • Practice	• Appearance • Body Language • Communication	• Positive Attitude • Professionalism • Follow-up

Prepare: The First Step Is Thorough Preparation.

a.   **Research:** Gain in-depth knowledge about the company, its culture, values, and recent achievements. Understand the job requirements and the industry landscape.

b. **Self-Assessment:** Identify your skills, strengths, and experiences that align with the job role. Be prepared to discuss your achievements and how they relate to the position.

c. **Practice:** Prepare responses to common interview questions, focusing on showcasing your skills and experiences. Conduct mock interviews to improve your communication and presentation skills.

Present: The second step is to present yourself confidently and professionally.

a. **Appearance:** Dress appropriately for the interview, ensuring a neat and professional appearance.

b. **Body Language:** Maintain good posture, make eye contact, and use confident gestures. Show enthusiasm and engage actively in the conversation.

c. **Communication:** Speak clearly and articulately, providing concise yet informative answers. Listen actively to the interviewer and respond thoughtfully.

Perform: The final step is to perform well during the interview.

a. **Positive Attitude:** Display a positive and enthusiastic attitude throughout the interview. Show genuine interest in the company and the position.

b. **Professionalism:** Display professionalism by being punctual, respectful, and attentive. Maintain a professional tone in your communication and avoid negative comments or excessive self-promotion.

c. **Follow-Up:** Send a thank you email or note to the interviewer within 24 hours, expressing your gratitude for the opportunity. Use this opportunity to reiterate your interest in the position and briefly summarise your qualifications.

By following this 3P model for interview success—Prepare, Present, and Perform—candidates can increase their chances of impressing the interviewer and securing the desired job opportunity.

Real-Life Case Study – From Failure to Success

Meet Deepak (name hidden), an ambitious and determined MBA student with a passion for finance and a dream of becoming a successful wealth adviser. Throughout his academic journey, Deepak consistently demonstrated his analytical and leadership abilities, earning good grades and accolades. However, when it came to job interviews, he faced multiple disappointments, leaving him feeling discouraged and questioning his potential.

Deepak's first job interviews with prominent Indian and multinational companies were nerve-wracking experiences. Despite his strong academic background and thorough preparation, he found himself stumbling over his answers and struggling to showcase his skills confidently. The interview panels sensed his nervousness, and unfortunately, he received rejections after each attempt.

Determined to turn things around, Deepak decided to seek guidance from a career coach. He understood that he needed personalised support and mentorship to address his interview challenges effectively. The coach's expertise in career development and interview preparation was exactly what Deepak needed to overcome his obstacles.

During his coaching sessions, Deepak and the coach identified his interview weaknesses and areas for improvement. They practised mock interviews, allowing Deepak to refine his responses and build his confidence. The coach also provided valuable insights and tips for presenting himself as a strong candidate during interviews.

With each coaching session, Deepak's interview skills improved significantly. He learned to articulate his strengths, share relevant experiences, and address difficult questions with poise. The coach's constructive feedback and encouragement helped Deepak develop a sense of self-assurance and belief in his abilities.

After several rounds of coaching and preparation, Deepak was ready to face another job interview. This time, he approached the interview with a newfound sense of assurance and self-belief. He answered questions with clarity and professionalism, leaving a lasting impression on the interviewers.

To Deepak's delight, he received a job offer from a multinational wealth management firm he had recently interviewed with. His dedication to self-improvement and the guidance of the coach had paid off.

PSYCHOMETRIC TESTS & OTHER ASSESSMENT TOOLS

With increasing competition in the job market, companies are increasingly using various tools, including psychometric tests, to assess and select the most suitable candidates during their hiring processes. For freshers entering the job market, these tests may be unfamiliar and intimidating. However, with adequate preparation and understanding of these assessments, you can significantly improve your chances of success. Let's explore some common psychometric tests used in fresher hiring and provide valuable insights on how to better prepare for these tests, enabling you to approach them with confidence and perform at your best.

APTITUDE TESTS

Aptitude tests are designed to evaluate your natural abilities and assess your potential to excel in specific tasks or job roles. These tests typically cover areas like numerical reasoning, verbal reasoning, logical reasoning, and abstract reasoning. They gauge your problem-solving skills, critical thinking abilities, and how well you can analyse information.

PREPARATION TIPS

Practise regularly with sample aptitude tests to familiarise yourself with the types of questions and time constraints.

- Strengthen your basic mathematical skills and improve your reading comprehension.

- Develop strategies to quickly analyse and solve problems during the test.

PERSONALITY ASSESSMENTS

Personality assessments aim to understand your behavioural traits, work preferences, and compatibility with the company's culture. These tests help employers determine if you possess the right personality attributes for the role and the team.

PREPARATION TIPS

- Be honest and authentic in your responses. Trying to manipulate your answers may lead to inconsistent results.

- Familiarise yourself with the traits and qualities most valued by the company you are applying to.

- Reflect on your own work preferences and values to gain a better understanding of yourself.

SITUATIONAL JUDGEMENT TESTS (SJTs)

SJTs present candidates with hypothetical workplace scenarios and ask how they would respond or act in each situation. These tests assess your decision-making skills, problem-solving abilities, and how well you can handle real-life work scenarios.

PREPARATION TIPS

- Review the company's values and code of conduct to align your responses with their organisational culture.

- Think critically about each scenario, considering the potential consequences of your chosen actions.

- Practice with sample SJTs to become familiar with the format and the types of challenges you might encounter.

BEHAVIOURAL INTERVIEWS

While not a traditional psychometric test, behavioural interviews assess your past behaviour and how you handled specific situations in previous experiences. Interviewers evaluate your responses to predict your future behaviour and performance.

PREPARATION TIPS

- Recall past experiences and prepare anecdotes that demonstrate key skills and competencies.

- Use the STAR (Situation, Task, Action, Result) method to structure your responses and provide clear examples.

- Focus on the positive outcomes and the skills you demonstrated in each situation.

CHAPTER 14

CHAMPIONING CASE-BASED INTERVIEWS & ART OF GROUP DISCUSSION

CASE-BASED INTERVIEWS

The case-based interview is a common method used to assess a candidate's problem-solving, analytical thinking, and decision-making skills. This chapter aims to equip you with the necessary knowledge and strategies to excel in case-based interviews. By understanding the structure, types of cases, and key preparation techniques, you can confidently approach these interviews and increase your chances of success.

UNDERSTANDING THE CASE-BASED INTERVIEW

STRUCTURE

Case-based interviews typically involve presenting a real or hypothetical business scenario to assess your ability to analyse the situation, identify relevant factors, and propose solutions. The interview may consist of one or more cases, followed by a discussion and evaluation of your approach.

TYPES OF CASES

1. **Business Cases:** These focus on solving business-related problems, such as market entry strategies, financial analysis, or operational challenges.

2. **Consulting Cases:** Commonly used in management consulting interviews, these cases require you to address complex business problems and provide strategic recommendations.

3. **Behavioural Cases:** These assess your decision-making skills by presenting ethical dilemmas or situations requiring you to demonstrate leadership and teamwork.

PREPARING FOR CASE-BASED INTERVIEWS

Case Study Practice:

a. Familiarise yourself with the case interview format by practising with sample cases from books, online resources, or casebooks provided by consulting clubs or career centres.

b. Develop a structured approach to analyse cases, such as the "MECE" (Mutually Exclusive, Collectively Exhaustive) framework, which helps you break down problems systematically.

MECE is a framework often used in problem-solving and structuring information. The MECE principle ensures that categories or elements you use to analyse a problem or data are distinct from one another (mutually exclusive) and that together, they cover all possible options (collectively exhaustive). This helps ensure that you don't overlap or miss any critical elements when addressing a problem.

Here's a simple example to illustrate MECE:

Problem: You're analysing the reasons for customer complaints about a new product.

Non-MECE Approach:

a. Product quality issues.

b. Customer service problems.

c. Shipping and delivery issues.

d. Price-related complaints.

In this non-MECE approach, the categories aren't mutually exclusive because a single complaint could involve multiple issues. For example, a customer could have a problem with both product quality and customer service. It's also not collectively exhaustive because there may be other reasons for complaints not covered in these categories.

MECE Approach:

1. Product quality issues.

    a. Defective items.

    b. Inaccurate product descriptions.

2. Customer service problems.

    a. Unresponsive support.

    b. Rude service.

3. Shipping and delivery issues.

    a. Late deliveries.

    b. Damaged items upon arrival.

4. Price-related complaints.

    a. High product cost.

    b. Hidden fees.

In the MECE approach, the categories are mutually exclusive because each complaint falls into only one category. They are also collectively exhaustive because these categories cover all possible reasons for customer complaints related to the new product. This structured approach allows for a more thorough analysis and a clearer understanding of the issues at hand.

Industry and Company Research:

a. Gain knowledge about the industry and company you are interviewing with. Understand their business model, market position, and recent developments.

b. Research case studies and industry-specific challenges to familiarise yourself with common issues faced by organisations in that sector.

Analytical Skills Development:

a. Enhance your quantitative and analytical skills through practice. Strengthen your ability to interpret data, perform calculations, and draw insights.

b. Brush up on business concepts, such as financial analysis, market research, and strategic frameworks, to build a solid foundation for approaching case problems.

Mock Interviews and Feedback:

a. Engage in mock case interviews with peers, mentors, or career advisers. Seek feedback on your problem-solving approach, communication style, and ability to structure your thoughts.

b. Take note of areas for improvement and refine your approach based on the feedback received.

Approaching the Case-Based Interview:

- **Understand the Problem:** Listen/Read carefully and clarify any uncertainties before proceeding. Ensure you have a clear understanding of the case problem, objectives, and any constraints provided.

- **Structure Your Approach:** Outline a clear structure to tackle the problem, identifying key areas to investigate. Communicate your framework to the interviewer before diving into the analysis.

- **Analyse the Case:** Collect relevant information by asking thoughtful and targeted questions. Utilise data provided in the case and ask for additional information if needed.

- **Use Critical Thinking and Creativity:** Apply critical thinking skills to analyse the information and identify patterns, trends, and potential solutions. Think creatively to generate innovative ideas or approaches that address the problem at hand.

- **Communicate Effectively:** Articulate your thoughts clearly, maintaining a logical flow of ideas. Summarise key insights, explain your reasoning, and support your conclusions with evidence. Engage with the interviewer by seeking their input, involving them in the discussion, and actively listening to their feedback.

Mastering the case-based interview requires a combination of knowledge, skills, and practice. Effective case-solving involves a structured approach, analytical thinking, clear communication, and adaptability. With dedication and practice, you can excel in these interviews.

Business Case: Expanding E-commerce Reach

Scenario:

You are a business consultant working with a retail company that specialises in selling clothing and accessories. The company has been successful in its brick-and-mortar stores but is looking to expand its reach and increase sales by establishing an online presence. They seek your expertise to develop a strategic plan for launching an e-commerce platform.

Case Prompt:

Develop a strategic plan for the company to successfully launch and manage an e-commerce platform. Consider factors such as target audience, website design and functionality, logistics and order fulfilment, marketing and customer acquisition, and post-launch evaluation and optimisation.

Solution:

Define Target Audience:

a. Conduct market research to identify the target audience for the company's online platform. Consider factors such as age, demographics, purchasing habits, and online shopping preferences.

b.   Tailor the website design, user experience, and product offerings to meet the needs and preferences of the target audience.

Website Design and Functionality:

a.   Design a user-friendly and visually appealing website that reflects the company's brand identity. Ensure easy navigation, clear product categorisation, and intuitive search functionality.

b.   Incorporate responsive design to provide a seamless experience across various devices, including desktops, tablets, and smartphones.

c.   Implement secure payment gateways and SSL certification to ensure customer data protection and build trust.

Logistics and Order Fulfilment:

a.   Establish partnerships with reliable logistics providers to handle order fulfilment, shipping, and returns efficiently.

b.   Implement a robust inventory management system to track stock levels, ensure timely product replenishment, and minimise the risk of stockouts.

c.   Optimise packaging and shipping processes to deliver products in a timely manner while maintaining quality and minimising costs.

Marketing and Customer Acquisition:

a.   Develop a comprehensive digital marketing strategy to drive traffic to the e-commerce platform. Utilise search engine optimisation (SEO), pay-per-click (PPC) advertising, social media marketing, and content marketing to increase brand visibility and attract potential customers.

b.   Implement targeted advertising campaigns to reach the identified target audience and maximise return on investment.

c. Leverage email marketing and personalised recommendations to nurture customer relationships and encourage repeat purchases.

Post-launch Evaluation and Optimisation:

a. Monitor key performance indicators (KPIs) such as website traffic, conversion rates, average order value, and customer satisfaction metrics.

b. Analyse data and feedback to identify areas of improvement and implement necessary optimisations to enhance the user experience, increase conversion rates, and drive customer loyalty.

c. Stay updated with industry trends and technological advancements to ensure the e-commerce platform remains competitive and aligned with customer expectations.

Conclusion:

By following this strategic plan, the retail company can successfully launch and manage an e-commerce platform, expanding its reach and increasing sales. A customer-centric approach, combined with effective website design, streamlined logistics, targeted marketing efforts, and continuous optimisation, will contribute to the success of the online venture. The company can leverage the opportunities presented by the digital landscape and establish a strong online presence, connecting with a broader customer base and driving long-term growth.

THE ART OF GROUP DISCUSSION

Group discussions play a crucial role in selection processes, including campus hiring, as they provide employers with insights into a candidate's communication skills, teamwork abilities, critical thinking, and leadership potential. However, it's important to note that group discussions are not only relevant for job interviews but also an essential life skill that can benefit individuals in various professional and personal situations. Mastering the art of group discussion not only enhances your academic and professional prospects but also develops essential life skills that can be applied in various situations.

Types of Group Discussions:

a. **Academic Group Discussions:** In educational settings, academic group discussions offer a platform to engage in intellectual debates, share perspectives, and critically analyse subjects related to your coursework. For example, you may discuss research papers, solve case studies, or debate current issues in your field of study. These discussions enhance your understanding of the subject matter and sharpen your analytical and communication skills.

b. **Professional Group Discussions:** In a professional context, group discussions are common for problem-solving, decision-making, and brainstorming sessions. These discussions aim to address organisational challenges, develop innovative solutions, and foster collaboration among team members. For instance, you may engage in discussions to develop strategies, analyse market trends, or assess project feasibility. Participating actively in such discussions showcases your ability to think critically, contribute ideas, and collaborate effectively.

c. **Selection Process Group Discussions:** Group discussions are frequently part of the selection process for educational institutes, internships, and job placements. During these discussions, candidates are given a topic or case study to discuss within a specified timeframe. The selection panel assesses your communication skills, ability to present logical arguments, teamwork, and leadership qualities. Excelling in these discussions can significantly enhance your chances of success in securing opportunities.

Practical Tips for Success in Group Discussions:

a. **Prepare Thoroughly:** Before the group discussion, research and gather relevant information on the given topic or case study. Develop a clear understanding of key points, different perspectives, and possible arguments. This preparation will enable you to contribute effectively during the discussion.

b. **Active Listening:** Actively listen to what others are saying during the discussion. Show genuine interest and maintain eye contact with the speaker. By actively listening, you demonstrate respect for others' opinions and create a conducive environment for collaboration and exchange of ideas.

c. **Constructive Communication:** Express your ideas clearly and concisely. Use appropriate language, tone, and non-verbal cues to convey your thoughts effectively. Be respectful of others' opinions and avoid interrupting or dominating the discussion. Engage in healthy debate and support your arguments with logical reasoning and evidence.

d. **Collaborate and Engage:** Foster a spirit of teamwork by encouraging others to participate and share their viewpoints. Acknowledge and appreciate different perspectives and ideas, even if they differ from your own. Build on others' thoughts and contribute to a constructive and collaborative discussion environment.

e. **Time Management:** Stay mindful of the allocated time for the group discussion. Pace yourself and ensure that you contribute meaningfully within the given timeframe. Avoid rambling or going off-topic, as it can derail the discussion and reflect poorly on your time management skills.

f. **Stay Calm and Confident:** Remain composed and confident throughout the discussion, even if you encounter opposing viewpoints or challenging questions. Maintain a positive demeanour, showcase your ability to handle pressure, and display self-assurance in your ideas and arguments.

g.	**Practice and Seek Feedback:** Engage in mock group discussions with peers or mentors to hone your skills. Seek feedback on your communication style, listening skills, and ability to collaborate. Use this feedback to improve and refine your approach for future discussions.

Avoid These Commonly Made Mistakes During Group Discussions:

During group discussions, it's important to be aware of common mistakes that students often make, as these can hinder their chances of success. Let's explore some of these mistakes and how you can avoid them:

a.	**Dominating the Discussion:**

One common mistake is dominating the discussion by speaking excessively and not giving others a chance to express their views. This can create an imbalance in the conversation and prevent meaningful contributions from other participants. Remember to give everyone an opportunity to share their thoughts and actively listen to their perspectives.

b.	**Lack of Preparation:**

Failing to prepare adequately for the group discussion can undermine your performance. It's essential to familiarise yourself with the topic or case study beforehand, gather relevant information, and Organise your thoughts. Preparation allows you to contribute confidently and substantiate your points effectively during the discussion.

c.	**Not Listening Actively:**

Listening is a crucial aspect of group discussions, but many students make the mistake of not listening actively. They may be too focused on formulating their response or waiting for their turn to speak. Active listening involves paying attention to others, understanding their viewpoints, and responding thoughtfully. Engage in the discussion with an open mind and show genuine interest in what others have to say.

d. **Being Overly Aggressive or Passive:**

Striking the right balance in your approach is essential during a group discussion. Being overly aggressive, interrupting others, or disregarding their opinions can create a hostile environment. On the other hand, being too passive and not actively participating can make your contributions less impactful. Aim for a collaborative and respectful approach, expressing your thoughts assertively while considering others' perspectives.

e. **Lack of Structure and Organisation:**

Presenting your ideas in a clear and organised manner is crucial for effective communication. Students often make the mistake of presenting their thoughts in a disorganised or rambling manner, which can make it difficult for others to follow their points. Take the time to structure your thoughts, present your ideas logically, and support them with relevant examples or evidence.

f. **Neglecting Non-Verbal Communication:**

Non-verbal communication plays a significant role in group discussions, and neglecting it can hinder your chances of success. Avoid negative body language, such as crossed arms or dismissive gestures, as it can create a barrier between you and other participants. Maintain eye contact, use appropriate facial expressions, and show active engagement through nodding and affirming gestures.

g. **Failure to Build on Others' Ideas:**

Group discussions are collaborative, and building on others' ideas is essential. Students often make the mistake of ignoring or dismissing others' contributions, missing opportunities for meaningful discussion and synergy. Actively engage with others' ideas, acknowledge their viewpoints, and offer constructive feedback or additions to enrich the conversation.

h. **Not Managing Time Effectively:**

Time management is crucial in group discussions, as there is often a limited time frame for the discussion. Students may make the mistake of going off-topic or spending too much time on a single point, leaving insufficient time for other aspects of the discussion. Be mindful of time constraints, stay focused on the topic, and encourage the group to stay on track.

By being aware of these common mistakes and taking steps to avoid them, you can enhance your performance in group discussions and increase your chances of success. Be respectful, prepared, and actively engaged, and you'll make a positive impression during these important interactions.

A Spectrum of Topics to Explore:

While the specific topics for group discussions can vary depending on the context and purpose, here are some broad categories of topics that students should consider preparing for:

1. **Current Affairs and Social Issues:**

Discussing current affairs and social issues allows participants to demonstrate their awareness of the world around them and their ability to critically analyse complex topics. Topics could include climate change, gender equality, technology's impact on society, or global political events.

2. **Ethical Dilemmas:**

Ethical dilemmas challenge participants to examine moral issues and make reasoned judgements. Topics could include debates on the ethics of artificial intelligence, animal testing, privacy in the digital age, or corporate social responsibility.

3. **Business and Management Case Studies:**

These discussions often involve analysing a given business scenario, identifying problems, and proposing solutions. Topics could revolve around market entry strategies, organisational change, crisis management, or ethical decision-making in business.

4. **Leadership and Teamwork:**

    Exploring topics related to leadership and teamwork allows participants to showcase their understanding of effective leadership styles, team dynamics, conflict resolution, and collaboration. Topics could include leadership in crises, diversity in teams, or the role of emotional intelligence in leadership.

5. **Technology and Innovation:**

    With technology playing a transformative role in various industries, discussions around technology and innovation are common. Topics could include the impact of artificial intelligence, the future of work in a digital world, cybersecurity challenges, or the ethical implications of emerging technologies.

6. **Education and Learning:**

    Topics related to education and learning enable participants to reflect on educational policies, teaching methods, and the future of education. Discussions could focus on the benefits of online learning, the role of technology in education, or the need for inclusive and equitable education systems.

7. **Cultural and Social Diversity:**

    These discussions delve into topics surrounding cultural diversity, inclusivity, and social justice. Topics could include racial equality, LGBTQ+ rights, cultural appropriation, or the role of media in shaping societal norms.

These are just a few examples, and the actual topics for group discussions will depend on the specific context. It's important to stay updated with current events, read widely, and engage in critical thinking to prepare for a variety of topics. Additionally, practising group discussions with peers can help you gain confidence and improve your ability to articulate your thoughts effectively.

HERE'S MY 4A MODEL FOR ACING A GROUP DISCUSSION

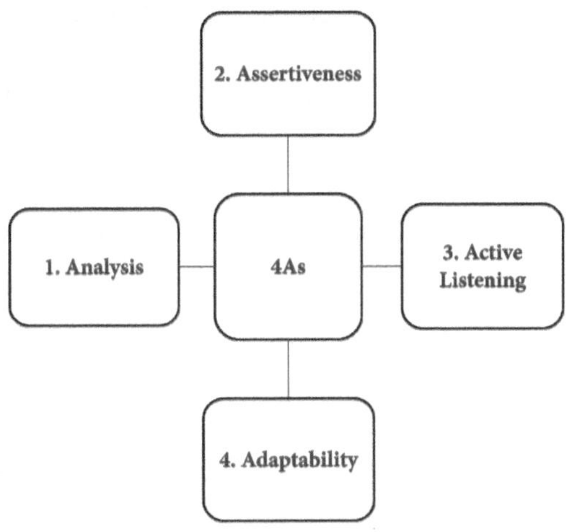

1. **Analysis:** Before participating in a group discussion, it is essential to analyse the topic or scenario at hand. Understand the key aspects, underlying issues, and various perspectives related to the topic. Conduct thorough research and gather relevant information to support your arguments during the discussion.

2. **Assertiveness:** Being assertive is crucial in a group discussion. Express your ideas and opinions confidently while respecting others' viewpoints. Clearly articulate your thoughts, provide logical reasoning, and back them up with examples or evidence. Maintain a balanced approach by considering different perspectives and finding common ground for effective collaboration.

3. **Active Listening:** Active listening is a fundamental aspect of successful group discussions. Pay attention to what others are saying, maintain eye contact, and show genuine interest in their viewpoints. Avoid interrupting or dominating the discussion. Take

notes to summarise important points raised by others and refer to them when presenting your own arguments.

4.   **Adaptability:** Group discussions often require adapting to the flow of the conversation and adjusting your approach accordingly. Be flexible in accepting new ideas, accommodating different viewpoints, and building upon others' contributions. Collaborate with fellow participants by actively engaging in dialogue, seeking clarifications, and building consensus when possible.

By following this 4 step approach—Analysis, Assertiveness, Active Listening, and Adaptability—you can enhance your performance in group discussions, effectively contribute to the conversation, and increase your chances of success.

CHAPTER 15

ALUMNI NETWORKS & CAREER SUPPORT

In your educational journey, alumni networks play a significant role in shaping your career. Alumni networks are communities of graduates who have walked the same path you are about to embark upon. They possess valuable knowledge, experiences, and connections that can provide you with invaluable career guidance, mentorship, and networking opportunities.

IMPORTANCE OF ALUMNI NETWORKS

Alumni networks serve as a bridge between your academic life and professional career. They provide a sense of belonging and camaraderie, connecting you with individuals who have gone through similar experiences and understand the challenges and opportunities that lie ahead. These networks can offer a wealth of resources, including alumni directories, online platforms, and alumni events, facilitating connections and fostering a supportive community. Here are some benefits of alumni networks:

1. **Career Guidance and Mentorship:**

   - **Job Referrals and Internship Opportunities:**

     Alumni networks often serve as a platform for job referrals and internship opportunities. Alumni who are aware of job openings or internships within their organisations or industries may prefer to hire or recommend qualified candidates from their alma mater. This gives you an advantage in the competitive job market, as you have the potential to access hidden job opportunities and secure referrals from alumni who can vouch for your capabilities.

- **Professional Development:**

  Alumni networks provide avenues for professional development through various initiatives and programmes. These can include workshops, seminars, webinars, and career fairs organised specifically for alumni. These events offer opportunities to enhance your skills, stay updated on industry trends, and learn from industry experts. Additionally, alumni may share their knowledge and experiences through guest lectures or panel discussions, providing valuable insights into the professional world.

- **Alumni Mentoring Programmes:**

  Many alumni networks have mentoring programmes that connect current students or recent graduates with experienced alumni. These mentorship programmes offer a structured framework for guidance, support, and advice on academic and career-related matters. Mentors can share their wisdom, provide feedback, and help mentees navigate challenges and make informed decisions. Having a mentor from your alumni network can significantly enhance your professional growth and development.

- **Lifelong Learning and Continuing Education:**

  Alumni networks often provide access to lifelong learning and continuing education opportunities. This can include discounted or exclusive access to online courses, professional certifications, or workshops. By leveraging these educational resources, you can acquire new skills, broaden your knowledge, and stay updated in your field of interest.

- **Alumni Contributions and Giving Back:**

  Being part of an alumni network allows you to contribute to your alma mater and give back to the educational institution that played a significant role in your personal and professional growth. You can contribute to scholarships, participate in alumni fundraising initiatives, volunteer for alumni events or committees, or share your expertise with current students. Giving back to your alma mater not only benefits the institution but also strengthens the bond between alumni and fosters a sense of pride and accomplishment.

  Engaging with your alumni network is a valuable investment in your professional journey. By actively participating in alumni activities, seeking mentorship, leveraging networking opportunities, and taking advantage of the resources available, you can tap into the collective knowledge, experiences, and support of your alumni community to enhance your career prospects and achieve long-term success.

2. **Networking Opportunities:**

   - **Access to a Vast Pool of Connections:** Alumni networks provide access to a diverse and extensive network of professionals who have graduated from your educational institution. This network can include individuals working in various industries, sectors, and geographic locations. By connecting with alumni, you gain access to their network of contacts, which can significantly expand your own professional connections.

   - **Industry Insights and Information:** Alumni who are already established in their careers can provide valuable insights into industry trends, job market dynamics, and professional development opportunities. By networking with alumni, you can gain valuable industry-specific information and stay updated on the latest developments in your field.

- **Hidden Job Markets:** Networking with alumni opens doors to hidden job markets that may not be publicly advertised. Many job opportunities are filled through referrals and personal connections. By tapping into the alumni network, you can gain access to job openings that may not be accessible through traditional job search methods.

- **Alumni Events and Online Communities:** Attending alumni events, such as reunions, conferences, or career fairs, provides opportunities to connect with alumni and expand your professional network. Additionally, joining online alumni communities or utilising alumni directories allows you to connect with alumni from different graduating classes and geographical locations, further expanding your network.

Networking with alumni is a powerful tool for career advancement and personal growth, and it is important to cultivate and nurture these connections throughout your professional life.

How to Leverage Your Alumni Connections

Proactively engaging with your alumni network can significantly enhance the benefits you derive from it. Here are some key points to consider when approaching your alumni network:

- **Introduce Yourself:** Reach out to alumni through professional networking platforms, email, or alumni events. Introduce yourself, mention your educational background, and express your interest in connecting with them. Be concise and clear in your communication, highlighting your enthusiasm to learn from their experiences.

- **Express Interest and Seek Advice:** Show genuine interest in their career paths and accomplishments. Ask thoughtful questions about their professional journey, challenges they faced, and lessons they learned. Seek their advice on navigating your own career path and inquire about any insights or guidance they can offer.

- **Inquire About Opportunities:** Politely inquire about any internship or job opportunities within their organisations or industry. Mention your skills and qualifications and express your interest in exploring potential openings. Remember to be respectful and understanding if they are unable to directly provide opportunities, as their role is to offer guidance and support.

- **Stay Connected:** Maintain regular communication with alumni who have provided valuable insights or connections. Keep them updated on your progress, achievements, and any changes in your career path. A genuine and consistent approach helps build lasting relationships within your alumni network.

- **Show Gratitude:** Remember to express gratitude for any guidance, mentorship, or opportunities provided by alumni. A simple thank you note or email can go a long way in building and nurturing these connections. Showing appreciation demonstrates professionalism and a genuine interest in maintaining the relationship.

Building relationships takes time and effort, so be patient, persistent, and proactive in nurturing these connections throughout your career journey.

ALUMNI CAREER SERVICES

Many educational institutions have dedicated career services departments that provide support to students and alumni. These departments offer a range of services, including job placement assistance, resume review, mock interviews, and career counselling. Take advantage of these resources to enhance your job search strategies, polish your professional

Here are some key points to consider regarding alumni career services:

a. **Job Placement Assistance:** Alumni career services often have strong connections with employers and industry professionals. They can provide you with job leads, internships, and other career opportunities. Make use of their resources and guidance to identify relevant job openings, enhance your application materials, and navigate the job market effectively.

b. **Resume Review and Cover Letter Assistance:** Career services can help you craft a compelling resume and cover letter that highlight your skills, experiences, and achievements. They can offer valuable feedback and suggestions to make your application materials stand out to potential employers.

c. **Mock Interviews and Interview Preparation:** Prepare for job interviews through mock interview sessions offered by career services. These practice sessions simulate real interview scenarios and allow you to refine your interview skills, improve your responses, and gain confidence. Additionally, career services can provide guidance on interview techniques, common interview questions, and strategies for showcasing your qualifications effectively.

d. **Career Counselling and Guidance:** Take advantage of career counselling sessions to explore different career paths, clarify your goals, and identify your strengths and interests. Career counsellors can provide personalised guidance, assess your skills and interests, and help you make informed decisions about your career trajectory.

e. **Professional Development Workshops and Events:** Alumni career services often Organise workshops, seminars, and networking events that focus on professional development. These events offer opportunities to enhance your skills, expand your knowledge, and network with professionals in your field of interest. Attend these events to gain industry insights, learn from experienced professionals, and connect with potential mentors.

f. **Online Career Resources:** Explore the online career resources provided by alumni career services. These resources may include job boards, networking platforms, webinars, and industry-specific resources. Use these resources to stay updated on job trends, gain industry insights, and access additional career-related support.

Remember to actively engage with alumni career services throughout your educational journey and beyond. Attend workshops, utilise their resources, and seek guidance whenever needed. By leveraging these services, you can enhance your job search strategies, develop key career skills, and make the most of your alumni network's support in achieving your professional goals.

Alumni networks play a crucial role in your career development journey. They offer a platform for connecting with experienced professionals, gaining insights into various industries, and accessing job opportunities. By actively engaging with alumni networks, leveraging connections, and seeking mentorship, you can enhance your professional growth and increase your chances of success in the competitive job market.

Remember, the power of alumni networks lies in the connections you build and the relationships you nurture. Approach alumni with respect, humility, and a genuine interest in learning from their experiences. Be proactive in reaching out, attending alumni events, and engaging in alumni communities. By tapping into the wealth of knowledge and support that alumni networks provide, you can propel your career forward and unlock new opportunities.

CHAPTER 16

PURSUING OVERSEAS EDUCATION

The trend of Indian students pursuing higher education abroad has gained significant momentum in recent times. While Indian higher education institutions continue to evolve and gain recognition on the global stage, a growing number of students are choosing to explore educational opportunities in countries such as the United States, the United Kingdom, Canada, and Australia. Based on my understanding this shift can be attributed to the below three factors:

1. **Broadening Horizons Through Global Exposure:**

   One compelling reason behind this trend is the desire for a broader and more globally diverse educational experience. Studying abroad offers Indian students a chance to step out of their comfort zones, engage with a culturally diverse student body, and gain exposure to international perspectives. It's an opportunity to explore new cultures, ideas, and ways of thinking that can profoundly enrich their academic and personal growth.

2. **Pathways to Settling Abroad:**

   Another driving force is the aspiration for international career prospects and potential immigration opportunities. Many Indian students see studying abroad as a pathway to not only obtaining a world-class education but also securing the possibility of settling down in their host countries. Acquiring a foreign degree can enhance their chances of landing desirable job opportunities and obtaining work visas or permanent residency status, thus opening doors to long-term international careers.

3. **The Influence of Trends and Peer Choices:**

    Admittedly, following the trend plays a role in this shift. The success stories of Indian students who have pursued higher education abroad and achieved significant milestones can inspire others to follow suit. Peer pressure and the desire to be part of a global academic community can influence some students' decisions. They may opt for studying abroad because it's considered prestigious and aligns with prevailing educational trends.

In this chapter we will delve into the benefits and challenges of pursuing education abroad, guiding you through the steps involved in selecting a suitable international institution, applying for visas, and adapting to a new cultural and academic environment. I am confident that by understanding these intricacies, you can make informed decisions and embark on a transformative educational journey.

BENEFITS OF STUDYING ABROAD

a. **Global Exposure:** Studying abroad exposes students to diverse cultures, languages, and perspectives, fostering intercultural competence and global awareness.

b. **Academic Excellence:** Many renowned international institutions offer world-class education, providing access to cutting-edge research, faculty expertise, and advanced facilities.

c. **Expanded Career Opportunities:** Studying abroad enhances students' employability by demonstrating their adaptability, cross-cultural communication skills, and global mindset to potential employers.

d. **Personal Growth:** Living in a foreign country challenges students to step out of their comfort zones, fostering independence, resilience, and self-confidence.

e. **Networking and Connections:** Studying abroad offers opportunities to build a global network of friends, classmates, and professionals from diverse backgrounds, creating lifelong connections.

Challenges of Studying Abroad

a. **Cultural Adjustment:** Adapting to a new cultural and social environment can be challenging. Students may experience culture shock, language barriers, and differences in academic expectations.

b. **Homesickness:** Being away from family and familiar surroundings can lead to feelings of homesickness. Developing coping strategies and seeking support from peers and university resources is important.

c. **Financial Considerations:** Studying abroad often comes with financial implications, including tuition fees, accommodation costs, and living expenses. Students should carefully plan and explore scholarship and funding opportunities.

d. **Visa and Immigration Processes:** Understanding the visa and immigration requirements of the chosen country is crucial. Students should research and adhere to the necessary procedures to obtain the required documentation.

e. **Academic Transitions:** Different education systems and teaching styles may require adjustments. Students should familiarise themselves with the academic expectations, grading systems, and learning methods of their host institution.

Selecting an International Institution

a. **Research:** Conduct thorough research on universities or colleges that offer programmes aligned with your academic interests and career goals. Consider factors such as reputation, accreditation, faculty expertise, and available resources.

b. **Programme Suitability:** Evaluate the curriculum, course structure, and academic support services of the programmes you are interested in. Ensure that they align with your academic and professional aspirations.

c. **Location:** Consider the country's cultural, social, and political environment, as well as its proximity to desired industries or career opportunities. Research the quality of life, safety, and cost of living in the chosen location.

d. **Financial Considerations:** Assess the tuition fees, scholarships, and potential living expenses to ensure that studying abroad is financially viable. Explore funding options and budget accordingly.

APPLYING FOR VISAS

When planning to pursue education abroad, understanding the visa requirements of the chosen country is of utmost importance. Each country has its own visa regulations and processes, and it is crucial to thoroughly research and comply with these requirements. Here are some key considerations:

a. **Research and Understand Visa Types:** Begin by researching the different visa types available for students. Common visa types for international students include student visas, study permits, or student residence permits. Understand the specific visa category that applies to your situation and the associated requirements.

b. **Be Mindful of Deadlines:** Visa application deadlines are critical, and missing them can jeopardise your plans for studying abroad. Familiarise yourself with the deadlines set by the embassy or consulate of the host country and ensure you submit your application well in advance to allow for processing time.

c. **Gather Necessary Documents:** Prepare all the required documents for your visa application. These may include proof of acceptance from the educational institution, financial statements demonstrating your ability to cover tuition fees and living expenses, health insurance coverage, a valid passport, and passport-sized photographs. Review the specific document requirements outlined by the embassy or consulate and ensure you have them in order before submitting your application.

d. **Seek Guidance:** It is highly recommended to consult the embassy or consulate of the host country to clarify any doubts and seek guidance on the visa application process. They can provide you with accurate information about the specific requirements, procedures, and any recent updates. Utilise online resources and official government websites for additional information and to stay up-to-date with any changes in visa regulations.

e. **Prepare for the Visa Interview:** In some cases, a visa interview may be required as part of the application process. Familiarise yourself with the interview process and potential questions that may be asked. Prepare your responses and gather any supporting documents that may be requested during the interview. Practice your interview skills to ensure you present yourself confidently and clearly.

f. **Be Financially Prepared:** Some countries may require proof of sufficient funds to cover your educational and living expenses during your stay. Prepare the necessary financial documents, such as bank statements or scholarship letters, to demonstrate your financial capacity.

g. **Follow Application Guidelines:** Carefully follow the application guidelines provided by the embassy or consulate. Pay attention to the specific instructions regarding the completion of forms, payment of fees, and submission methods. Double-check your application to ensure all information is accurate and complete.

It is essential to start the visa application process early to allow for any unforeseen delays and to ensure a smooth transition to your host country. Stay organised, remain patient throughout the process, and seek assistance whenever needed.

Adapting to a New Cultural and Academic Environment:

a. **Cultural Orientation:** Familiarise yourself with the local customs, traditions, and etiquette of the host country. Learn basic phrases in the local language to facilitate communication.

b. **Support Systems:** Seek support from international student services, student organisations, and mentors at your host institution. They can provide guidance and advice, and help you navigate the challenges of adjusting to a new environment.

c. **Engage in Cultural Activities:** Participate in cultural events, join clubs or societies, and interact with local students to enhance your cultural understanding and make new connections.

d. **Time Management and Study Skills:** Adapt to academic expectations and develop effective time management and study skills. Seek assistance from academic support services if needed.

e. **Health and Well-being:** Prioritise your physical and mental well-being. Familiarise yourself with the healthcare system of the host country, maintain a balanced lifestyle, and seek support if you experience any challenges.

Language Preparation:

Language preparation is a crucial aspect of studying abroad, particularly when the destination country has a different primary language. Adequate language skills not only facilitate academic success but also enhance cultural immersion and the overall experience of living in a foreign country. In this section, we will delve into the significance of language preparation and provide valuable guidance on how you can enhance your language skills before and during your study abroad experience.

a. **Recognising the Importance of Language Preparation:**

Studying in a foreign country requires you to navigate daily life, academic settings, and social interactions in a different language. Proficiency in the local language not only facilitates communication but also opens doors to a deeper understanding of the culture, smoother integration with the local community, and the ability to fully engage in your academic coursework. It also enables you to seize opportunities such as internships or part-time jobs that may require proficiency in the local language.

b. **Utilising Language Learning Resources:**

There are numerous resources available to support your language learning journey. Explore language learning apps, online platforms, and language exchange programmes that offer interactive lessons, vocabulary drills, grammar exercises, and conversation practice. Language learning software like Duolingo, Rosetta Stone, or Babbel can be valuable tools to enhance your language skills at your own pace.

c. **Engaging in Language Proficiency Tests:**

Many study abroad programmes and universities require proof of language proficiency. Familiarise yourself with commonly accepted language proficiency tests such as TOEFL (Test of English as a Foreign Language) or IELTS (International English Language Testing System). Understand the test registration process, and the structure of the tests, and explore available preparation materials to help you achieve your desired scores.

d. **Preparing in Advance:**

It is advisable to start your language preparation well in advance of your study abroad journey. Allocate dedicated time for language learning, set achievable goals, and create a study plan. Immerse yourself in the language through online resources, language exchange partners, or language courses to build a solid foundation before arriving in the host country.

e. **Immersion and Practice:**

Studying abroad provides a unique opportunity for immersive language practice. Embrace the local language by practising with native speakers, participating in language exchange programmes, and joining language clubs or conversation groups. Engaging with the local community allows for the practical application of your language skills and promotes cultural integration.

f. **Taking Advantage of Language Support Services:**

Be aware of the language support services available at your host institution, such as language centres, tutoring programmes, or language conversation partners. These resources provide additional support tailored to the specific needs of international students. They offer guidance, feedback, and practice opportunities to help you improve your language skills.

g. **Cultivating a Growth Mindset:**

Learning a new language can be challenging, and it's normal to encounter setbacks or frustrations along the way. Adopt a growth mindset, viewing language learning as a continuous process of improvement. Embrace mistakes as valuable learning opportunities and maintain determination and resilience throughout your language learning journey.

By recognising the significance of language preparation and utilising the practical guidance provided on language learning resources, proficiency tests, and strategies for enhancing your language skills, you can approach your study abroad experience with confidence and effectively communicate in a foreign language. Embrace the opportunity to immerse yourself in a new language and culture, and make the most of your study abroad journey.

CHOOSING THE RIGHT TIMING FOR YOUR OVERSEAS EDUCATION

Deciding when to pursue higher education abroad, whether for undergraduate or postgraduate studies, is an important consideration that requires thoughtful evaluation. Let's explore the pros and cons of both options to help you make an informed decision.

Pros of Pursuing Undergraduate Studies Abroad:

a. **Exposure to a Global Learning Environment:** Studying abroad for your undergraduate degree allows you to experience a diverse and multicultural learning environment. You can interact with students from various backgrounds, gain global perspectives, and broaden your horizons.

b. **Early Exposure to Independence:** Going abroad at a younger age gives you the opportunity to develop independence and adaptability. It encourages personal growth, enhances your problem-solving skills, and helps you become more self-reliant.

c. **Building a Strong Foundation:** Pursuing your undergraduate degree abroad can provide a solid academic foundation in your chosen field. Many universities offer comprehensive undergraduate programmes that combine theoretical knowledge with practical experiences, setting you up for success in your future career.

d. **Networking Opportunities:** Studying abroad allows you to build a global network of friends, classmates, and industry professionals. These connections can be invaluable for future collaborations, job opportunities, and personal growth.

Cons of Pursuing Undergraduate Studies Abroad:

a. **Financial Considerations:** Studying abroad for your undergraduate degree can be expensive. Tuition fees, living expenses, and travel costs need to be carefully evaluated, and financial support options such as scholarships or student loans should be explored.

b. **Limited Academic Specialisation:** Undergraduate programmes abroad often provide a broader education, allowing you to explore various subjects before choosing a specific major. If you already have a clear career path or a specific area of interest, you might prefer to pursue specialised studies at a later stage.

c. **Adjustment and Homesickness:** Moving to a different country at a young age can be challenging. Adjusting to a new culture, language, and educational system might take time, and homesickness can be a common experience. It's important to be prepared for these emotional and social adjustments.

Pros of Pursuing Postgraduate Studies Abroad:

a. **Specialisation and Career Advancement:** Pursuing a postgraduate degree abroad allows you to specialise in your field of interest and gain advanced knowledge and skills. This can enhance your career prospects and open doors to higher-level positions.

b. **Research Opportunities:** Many universities abroad offer state-of-the-art research facilities and resources for postgraduate students. Engaging in research projects can deepen your understanding of your chosen field and contribute to advancements in your area of study.

c. **Networking and Global Connections:** Studying at the postgraduate level provides excellent networking opportunities. Interacting with professors, researchers, and fellow students from around the world can expand your professional network and expose you to diverse perspectives.

d. **Cultural Immersion and Personal Growth:** Pursuing postgraduate studies abroad allows you to immerse yourself in a new culture and develop a broader worldview. It challenges you to step out of your comfort zone, fosters personal growth, and promotes intercultural understanding.

Cons of Pursuing Postgraduate Studies Abroad:

- **Higher Financial Investment:** Postgraduate programmes abroad tend to have higher tuition fees compared to undergraduate programmes. You need to consider the financial implications, including the cost of living, accommodation, and any additional expenses associated with your studies.

- **Competitiveness and Admission Criteria:** Admission into postgraduate programmes abroad can be highly competitive. You need to meet the specific academic and language proficiency requirements of your chosen university or programme. Additionally, securing funding or scholarships for postgraduate studies can be more challenging.

- **Limited Flexibility:** Pursuing postgraduate studies abroad might require you to commit to a specific programme and university for a longer duration. This might limit your flexibility in terms of exploring other opportunities or pursuing a career directly after completing your undergraduate degree.

Ultimately, the decision to pursue undergraduate or postgraduate studies abroad depends on your individual goals, preferences, and circumstances. Consider factors such as your academic interests, career aspirations, financial situation, and personal readiness for an international experience. Research and evaluate various universities and programmes to find the best fit for your educational journey.

CHAPTER 17

MASTERING COMPETITIVE EXAMS— STRATEGIES FOR SUCCESS

Competitive exams play a significant role in the education system of India, especially for entrance into professional courses and government jobs. These exams, such as the CDS (Combined Defence Services), UPSC (Union Public Service Commission), and SSC (Staff Selection Commission) exams, serve as gateways to prestigious institutions and lucrative career opportunities. They require focused preparation, effective time management, and access to appropriate resources.

The significance of competitive exams lies in their ability to assess candidates' knowledge, aptitude, and problem-solving skills. These exams are designed to select the best candidates based on merit, ensuring a fair and transparent selection process. They serve as benchmarks of excellence and provide opportunities for individuals to showcase their abilities and secure admission or employment in their desired fields.

Preparing for Competitive Exams

To effectively prepare for competitive exams, it is essential to adopt a strategic approach. Here are some guidance and strategies to enhance your preparation:

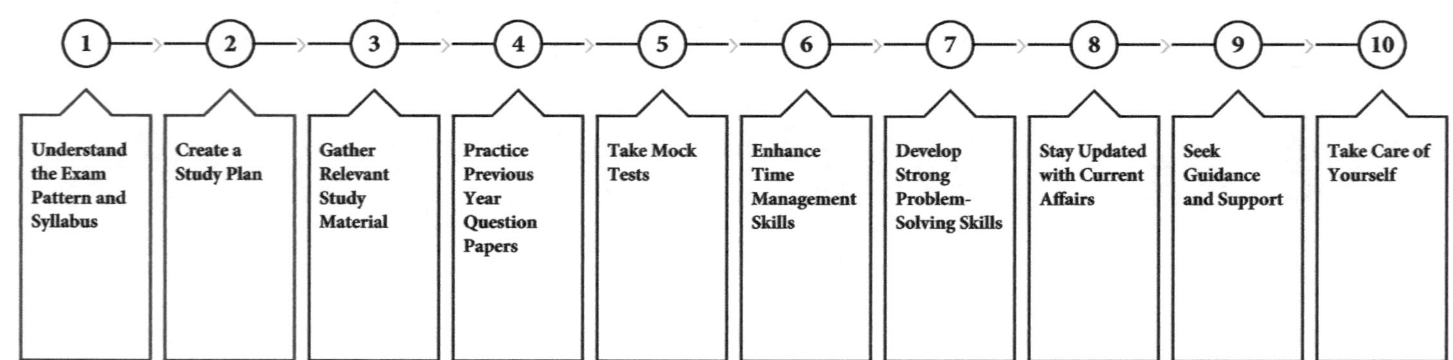

a. **Understand the Exam Pattern and Syllabus:** Begin by thoroughly understanding the exam pattern, including the number of sections, duration, marking scheme, and question formats. Familiarise yourself with the syllabus to identify the topics and subjects that need to be covered.

b. **Create a Study Plan:** Develop a comprehensive study plan that allocates sufficient time for each subject and topic. Set realistic goals and establish a study routine that incorporates regular revisions, practice sessions, and mock tests. Consider your strengths and weaknesses while allocating time for different subjects.

c. **Gather Relevant Study Material:** Identify reliable and updated study resources, such as textbooks, reference books, online courses, and study materials provided by coaching institutes. Make sure to choose resources that align with the exam syllabus and cover all essential topics.

d. **Practice Previous Year Question Papers:** Solving previous year question papers provides insights into the exam pattern, helps you understand the types of questions asked, and familiarises you with the level of difficulty. It also allows you to identify areas where you need more practice and helps improve your time management skills.

e. **Take Mock Tests:** Mock tests simulate the actual exam environment and help you evaluate your performance. They provide an opportunity to assess your strengths and weaknesses, identify areas for improvement, and refine your exam-taking strategies. Analyse your performance in mock tests and focus on areas that need more attention.

f. **Enhance Time Management Skills:** Time management is crucial during competitive exams. Practice solving questions within the stipulated time frame to improve your speed and accuracy. Divide your time strategically among different sections or subjects based on their weightage and your proficiency.

g. **Develop Strong Problem-Solving Skills:** Competitive exams often require analytical and problem-solving skills. Enhance your problem-solving abilities by practising a wide range of questions and developing logical thinking and reasoning skills. Solve puzzles, practice mathematical calculations, and work on developing a systematic approach to problem-solving.

h. **Stay Updated with Current Affairs:** Stay updated with current affairs, national and international events, government policies, and recent developments. Read newspapers, magazines, and online sources to stay informed. This knowledge is crucial for exams that include a current affairs section.

i. **Seek Guidance and Support:** Consider enrolling in coaching programmes or online courses that specialise in preparing students for specific competitive exams. These programmes provide expert guidance, study materials, practice tests, and personalised feedback. Additionally, seek guidance from mentors, teachers, or experienced candidates who have successfully cleared similar exams.

j. **Take Care of Yourself:** While exam preparation is crucial, it is equally important to take care of your physical and mental well-being. Maintain a balanced lifestyle, get sufficient sleep, exercise regularly, and take breaks to relax and rejuvenate. Manage stress through techniques like meditation, deep breathing exercises, and maintaining a positive mindset.

Remember, each individual's preparation strategy may vary based on their strengths, weaknesses, and preferences. It is important to develop a personalised approach that suits your learning style and aligns with your goals.

In conclusion, competitive exams in India hold great significance in determining admission and employment opportunities. Effective preparation, time management, and access to relevant resources are key factors for success. By following a systematic study plan, practising consistently, and seeking guidance when needed, you can enhance your chances of performing well in these exams and achieving your desired goals.

ROLE OF COACHING INSTITUTES

When it comes to preparing for competitive exams, coaching institutes can be instrumental in boosting your chances of success. Before making a decision to invest in a coaching institute, it's important to consider the advantages and disadvantages they offer. Let's explore these factors to help you make an informed choice:

ADVANTAGES

a. **Structured Approach:** Coaching institutes provide a structured approach to exam preparation, covering the entire syllabus systematically. They offer a well-defined study plan, time management strategies, and a roadmap for success.

b. **Expert Faculty:** Coaching institutes employ experienced and knowledgeable faculty members who specialise in the subjects included in the exam. These experts have a deep understanding of the exam pattern, marking scheme, and important topics, and they can provide valuable insights and guidance.

c. **Comprehensive Study Materials:** Coaching institutes provide comprehensive study materials that are specifically designed for the exam. These materials cover all the necessary concepts, formulas, and techniques required to excel in the exam. They save students time and effort in collecting and organising study materials.

d. **Regular Mock Tests:** Coaching institutes conduct regular mock tests that simulate the actual exam environment. These tests help students become familiar with the exam pattern, time constraints, and the pressure of the exam. They also provide an opportunity for students to assess their performance, identify areas of improvement, and fine-tune their exam-taking strategies.

e. **Peer Learning and Motivation:** Coaching institutes bring together a group of aspirants who share a common goal. This creates an environment of peer learning and healthy competition, where students can exchange ideas, discuss difficult concepts, and motivate each other. It can foster a sense of camaraderie and support, making the preparation journey more enjoyable.

DISADVANTAGES

a. **Cost:** Joining a coaching institute can be expensive, and it may not be affordable for everyone. Tuition fees, study materials, and additional expenses can add up, putting financial strain on students and their families.

b. **Time Commitment:** Coaching institutes often have fixed schedules, and students are required to attend classes regularly. This can be challenging for students who have other commitments, such as part-time jobs, family responsibilities, or involvement in extracurricular activities.

c. **One-size-fits-all Approach:** Coaching institutes cater to a large number of students, and their teaching methods may not cater to the individual needs and learning styles of every student. Some students may require more personalised attention or have unique learning preferences that may not be adequately addressed in a group setting.

d. **Dependency:** Relying solely on coaching institutes for exam preparation can create a dependency on external guidance. Students may become overly reliant on the coaching institute's study materials and strategies, which may limit their ability to develop independent thinking and problem-solving skills.

e. **Variation in Quality:** Not all coaching institutes are equal in terms of quality and effectiveness. Some institutes may have a more established reputation, experienced faculty, and a proven track record of success, while others may not meet the same standards. It is important for students to thoroughly research and choose a reputable coaching institute.

The success rate of coaching institutes can vary depending on various factors, including the quality of the institute, the dedication and effort put in by students, and the competitiveness of the exam itself. It is important to note that success in competitive exams is not solely dependent on coaching institutes. Candidates still need to put in their own hard work, perseverance, and continuous self-study.

While coaching institutes can provide guidance, study materials, and a structured approach to preparation, it is ultimately the candidate's efforts and abilities that determine their success. Success rates can differ significantly from one coaching institute to another and can also vary among different exams.

It is recommended that students consider the advantages and disadvantages of coaching institutes and assess their own learning preferences, resources, and needs before making a decision. It is also important to remember that coaching institutes are not the only path to success in competitive exams. Many candidates have achieved remarkable results through self-study, online resources, and dedicated practice.

Ultimately, candidates should evaluate their own strengths, weaknesses, and preferences, and choose a preparation method that aligns with their individual circumstances and goals. It is essential to strike a balance between external guidance and self-study and to focus on continuous learning and improvement throughout the preparation journey.

CHAPTER 18

SCHOLARSHIPS AND FINANCIAL AID

Meet Sudip, a young and spirited student who has just finished his high school journey. But as he stands at this pivotal crossroad in life, Sudip has something special on his mind — a dream that flickers like the brightest star in the night sky. His dream? To pursue a bachelor's degree in computer science at one of India's prestigious universities.

Sudip's dream isn't just his alone; it's a dream shared by countless Indian youth, both in small towns and sprawling cities. It's the dream of reaching the pinnacle of knowledge and expertise in a field that ignites their passion. It's the dream of achieving greatness through education. But there's one looming obstacle that threatens to cast a shadow over Sudip's dreams – the formidable cost of education. With the tuition fees, textbooks, living expenses, and other academic necessities piling up, Sudip's parents worry about how they'll manage to support their son's academic aspirations.

In this chapter, we embark on a journey alongside Sudip to unravel the mysteries of education loans and sponsorships. We'll navigate the complex landscape of financing higher education, and most importantly, we'll learn how finances should never be the roadblock to the success of an ambitious student.

This chapter explores the various scholarship opportunities and financial assistance options available to help alleviate the financial burden of education. By providing advice on researching and applying for scholarships, grants, and educational loans, this chapter aims to empower students to access the financial resources they need to pursue their academic aspirations.

UNDERSTANDING SCHOLARSHIPS AND FINANCIAL AID

In today's educational landscape, scholarships and financial aid play a crucial role in making education more accessible and affordable for students. This section aims to provide a comprehensive understanding of scholarships and financial aid, highlighting their significance in supporting students' educational pursuits.

TYPES OF SCHOLARSHIPS

Scholarships come in various forms, and it is important for students to understand the different types available to them. This section explains three main categories of scholarships:

Merit-Based Scholarships	Need-Based Scholarships	Government Scholarships	Institution-Specific Scholarships	International Scholarships	Research Scholarships

a. **Merit-Based Scholarships:** These scholarships are awarded to students based on their academic achievements, such as high grades or ranking in competitive exams. They recognise and reward students for their exceptional performance and provide financial assistance to pursue higher education.

b. **Need-Based Scholarships:** Need-based scholarships are awarded to students who demonstrate financial need. These scholarships aim to make education accessible to students from low-income backgrounds by providing financial support to cover tuition fees, living expenses, and other educational costs.

c. **Government Scholarships:** Various government schemes and policies in India provide scholarships for higher education.

Examples include the National Means-cum-Merit Scholarship Scheme (NMMSS), the Central Sector Scheme of Scholarships for College and University Students, and the Post-Matric Scholarship Scheme for SC/ST/OBC/Minority students. These scholarships are usually based on merit or socio-economic criteria.

d. **Institution-Specific Scholarships:** Many educational institutions, both in India and abroad, offer scholarships to attract and support talented students. These scholarships may be based on academic merit, extracurricular achievements, or specific criteria set by the institution.

e. **International Scholarships:** Several organisations and governments around the world offer scholarships for Indian students to pursue higher education abroad. Examples include the Fulbright Scholarship, Commonwealth Scholarships, and various country-specific scholarships. These scholarships provide opportunities for Indian students to study abroad and gain international exposure.

f. **Research Scholarships:** Research scholarships are available for students pursuing research-oriented programmes, such as Ph.D. or M.Phil. These scholarships support students in their research endeavours by covering tuition fees and research expenses and providing a stipend.

It is important to note that the availability, eligibility criteria, and application processes for scholarships, grants, and loans may vary. Students are advised to research and identify relevant opportunities through official government websites, educational institutions, scholarship search engines, and trusted resources. It is also recommended to read and understand the terms and conditions of each scholarship or loan programme before applying.

GRANTS AND LOANS

In addition to scholarships, there are grants and loans as financial aid options. Grants are similar to scholarships, as they do not need to be repaid. They are typically awarded based on financial needs or specific criteria set by the funding organisation or institution. On the other hand, loans are financial resources that need to be repaid over time. Educational loans are specifically designed to help students cover the costs of tuition, books, and other educational expenses.

a. **Grants and Fellowships:** Grants and fellowships are similar to scholarships but often come with additional benefits, such as research funding, travel allowances, and mentorship opportunities. They are typically awarded to students pursuing specific fields of study or engaged in research projects.

b. **Educational Loans:** In addition to scholarships and grants, educational loans are a common financial aid option for higher education. Banks and financial institutions provide loans specifically designed for educational purposes. These loans cover tuition fees, living expenses, and other educational costs. They often have favourable interest rates and flexible repayment options.

Let's delve into the different types of educational loans available and the associated terms and conditions:

- **Government-Funded Educational Loans:** The Government of India offers various loan schemes to support students pursuing higher education. One such scheme is the Central Sector Interest Subsidy Scheme (CSIS), which provides interest subsidies on educational loans for economically weaker sections of society. Under this scheme, the government bears the interest on the loan during the moratorium period. Another scheme is the Pradhan Mantri Vidya Lakshmi Karyakram, a web-based portal that provides a single-window platform for students to apply for educational loans from multiple banks.

- **Bank Loans:** Banks in India offer educational loans to finance higher education. These loans cover tuition fees, accommodation costs, travel expenses, and other educational-related expenses. Banks typically have their own terms and conditions, interest rates, and repayment periods. It is advisable to compare loan offerings from different banks and choose the one that best suits your needs. Banks may require collateral or a guarantor, depending on the loan amount.

- **Private Loans:** Private financial institutions also provide educational loans for higher education. These loans may have different interest rates, repayment periods, and eligibility criteria compared to government-funded loans and bank loans. Private loans are often more flexible in terms of loan amount and repayment options but may have higher interest rates. It is essential to carefully review the terms and conditions of private loans and ensure that they align with your financial situation and plans.

TERMS AND CONDITIONS OF EDUCATIONAL LOANS

- **Interest Rates:** Educational loans may have fixed or floating interest rates. It is important to understand the applicable interest rate, as it will determine the total cost of the loan over the repayment period. Some government-funded loans may offer subsidised interest rates or interest rate concessions based on specific criteria.

- **Repayment Period:** The repayment period for educational loans varies depending on the loan amount and the terms set by the lending institution. It is crucial to consider the repayment period and ensure that it aligns with your financial capability and plans.

- **Moratorium Period:** Most educational loans have a moratorium period, during which borrowers are not required to make repayments. This period typically extends to the duration of the course and a specific period afterward. Understanding the moratorium period is essential, as it allows students to focus on their studies without the immediate burden of loan repayment.

⅄ **Loan Forgiveness Options:** Some loan schemes may offer loan forgiveness or repayment assistance options. For example, government-funded loans may have provisions for loan forgiveness if the borrower meets certain criteria, such as working in specific sectors or underserved areas. It is important to explore such options and understand the eligibility criteria.

When considering an educational loan, it is advisable to research and compare the terms and conditions offered by different lenders. Factors such as interest rates, repayment periods, flexibility, and additional benefits should be carefully evaluated. Additionally, understanding the repayment process and planning for loan repayment in advance can help ensure a smooth financial journey after completing your education.

Remember to read and comprehend the loan agreement thoroughly, seek clarification from the lender if needed, and make informed decisions based on your financial circumstances and future aspirations.

SIGNIFICANCE OF SCHOLARSHIPS AND FINANCIAL AID

The significance of scholarships and financial aid cannot be overstated when it comes to making education more accessible and affordable for students like you. In this section, we will delve into the importance of scholarships and financial aid, and how they can positively impact your educational journey.

First and foremost, scholarships and financial aid are essential in alleviating the financial burden on you and your family. By providing financial support, scholarships and aid enable you to focus on your studies and personal development without constantly worrying about the cost of education. This relief allows you to fully immerse yourself in your academic pursuits and make the most of your learning experience.

Moreover, scholarships and financial aid contribute to creating a more inclusive and diverse educational environment. They provide opportunities for students from various socio-economic backgrounds, cultures, and communities to pursue higher education. Regardless of your financial circumstances, scholarships and aid ensure that you have equal access to quality education, promoting a fair and equitable educational system.

Furthermore, scholarships and financial aid recognise and reward your academic achievements, talents, and potential. They serve as a proof of your hard work and dedication, motivating and inspiring you to continue excelling in your academic pursuits. By providing this recognition and support, scholarships and aid foster a culture of meritocracy and excellence, encouraging you to strive for your best and reach your full potential.

Understanding the significance of scholarships and financial aid is crucial for your educational journey. In this section, I have provided you with a comprehensive overview of the different types of scholarships, grants, and loans available. By familiarising yourself with these options, you can make informed decisions, explore relevant opportunities, and pursue your educational goals with the necessary financial support. Remember, scholarships and financial aid are not only about relieving the financial burden but also about recognising your potential and providing equal access to education for all.

RESEARCHING SCHOLARSHIP OPPORTUNITIES

As you start your search for scholarships, it's crucial to adopt effective research strategies to maximise your chances of finding suitable opportunities. This section provides guidance on how to conduct thorough research and discover scholarship options that align with your needs and qualifications.

- **Start by exploring multiple sources:** Government websites, scholarship portals, philanthropic organisations, and educational institutions are excellent resources to begin your search. These platforms often provide comprehensive information about various scholarships available to students. Take the time to browse through their databases and familiarise yourself with the opportunities that suit your field of study, academic achievements, and personal circumstances.

- **Consider eligibility criteria and requirements:** Each scholarship has specific eligibility criteria, such as academic merit, financial need, community involvement, or specific demographic criteria. As you research scholarships, pay close attention to these requirements to ensure you meet the necessary qualifications. Be honest with yourself about your eligibility for each opportunity, as this will save you time and effort in the application process.

- **Keep track of application deadlines:** Scholarship deadlines can vary significantly, so it's crucial to create a timeline or use a planner to keep track of application deadlines. Missing deadlines can result in missed opportunities, so make sure you note down the dates and plan your application process accordingly. Setting reminders and working on your applications well in advance will help you stay organised and submit your materials on time.

- **Prepare required documents:** Scholarships typically require certain documents, such as academic transcripts, recommendation letters, essays, or financial statements. As you research scholarships, make note of the required documents for each application. Take the time to gather these documents and ensure they are prepared well in advance. This will save you from last-minute stress and allow you to present your application in the best possible way.

Remember, researching scholarship opportunities requires patience and diligence. It's important to dedicate time to this process and be thorough in your search. By exploring multiple sources, considering eligibility criteria, noting application deadlines, and preparing the required documents, you will be well-prepared to pursue scholarships that can provide valuable financial support for your higher education journey.

Keep in mind that scholarship opportunities can be highly competitive, so it's important to give your best effort in preparing your applications. Take the time to tailor your application materials, highlight your strengths, and showcase your passion and dedication. With careful research and a well-crafted application, you increase your chances of securing scholarships that can significantly contribute to your educational aspirations.

Applying for Scholarships

When it comes to applying for scholarships, attention to detail and careful preparation are key. This section offers step-by-step guidance on the scholarship application process, ensuring that you navigate the process successfully and maximise your chances of securing financial support for your education.

- **Follow the application instructions:** Each scholarship has its own set of application instructions, and it's crucial to carefully read and understand them before you begin the application process. Pay close attention to the requirements, deadlines, and any specific guidelines provided by the scholarship provider. Following these instructions demonstrates your attention to detail and commitment to the application process.

- **Organise your documents:** Before you start filling out the application, gather all the necessary documents. These may include academic transcripts, proof of enrolment, personal identification documents, recommendation letters, and personal statements. Keep these documents in a secure and easily accessible location to ensure you have everything you need when completing your application.

- **Craft a compelling personal statement:** Many scholarships require a personal statement or essay that allows you to express your goals, aspirations, and reasons for applying. Take the time to carefully craft a well-written and compelling personal statement. Highlight your achievements, experiences, and how the scholarship will contribute to your academic and career goals. Tailor your personal statement to the specific requirements and values of each scholarship, showcasing your unique qualities and passion.

- **Obtain strong recommendation letters:** Most scholarship applications require recommendation letters from teachers, mentors, or professionals who can attest to your character, academic abilities, and potential. Choose individuals who know you well and can provide specific examples of your accomplishments and strengths. Reach out to them well in advance, providing them with ample time to write thoughtful and detailed letters of recommendation.

- **Highlight academic and extracurricular achievements:** Scholarships often consider academic performance and involvement in extracurricular activities. Take the opportunity to showcase your achievements, awards, leadership roles, community service, and other notable contributions. Provide evidence of your dedication, commitment, and the positive impact you have made in your academic and extracurricular pursuits.

- **Proofread and review your application:** Before submitting your application, thoroughly review it for any errors, typos, or inconsistencies. Proofread your personal statement, check that all documents are properly attached, and ensure that you have followed all instructions accurately. Seek feedback from teachers, mentors, or family members to get a fresh perspective and make necessary improvements.

- **Submit your application on time:** Meeting application deadlines is crucial for scholarship consideration. Aim to submit your application well before the deadline to avoid any last-minute technical issues or delays. Take note of any additional steps required, such as mailing hard copies or submitting online forms, and ensure that you complete these tasks within the specified time frame.

Applying for scholarships is a competitive process, and attention to detail is crucial. By carefully following the application instructions, organising your documents, crafting a compelling personal statement, obtaining strong recommendation letters, and showcasing your academic and extracurricular achievements, you increase your chances of standing out among other applicants. It's important to approach the application process with enthusiasm and a positive mindset. Even if you face rejection, remember that it's part of the process, and there are numerous scholarship opportunities available. Keep refining your application materials, seeking feedback, and exploring additional scholarships to increase your chances of success.

GOVERNMENT POLICIES AND SCHEMES

Within the realm of scholarships and financial aid, it's important to be aware of the various government policies and schemes that exist to support students in securing financial assistance for their education. This chapter explores these initiatives, providing valuable information on the eligibility criteria, application process, and benefits associated with each.

One notable initiative is the National Scholarship Portal (NSP)-(https://scholarships.gov.in/) which serves as a centralised platform for students to apply for multiple scholarships offered by different government departments and organisations. The NSP simplifies the application process and allows students to access a wide range of scholarships through a single portal.

Another prominent government scheme is the Prime Minister's Scholarship Scheme, (india.gov.in) which aims to provide financial assistance to the wards of ex-servicemen pursuing professional courses. This scheme recognises the sacrifices made by the armed forces and offers support to their families in pursuing higher education.

Additionally, the Post-Matric Scholarship (http://www.pmsonline. bih.nic.in/) and Merit-cum-Means Scholarship are schemes that focus on providing financial aid to students from economically disadvantaged backgrounds. These schemes aim to ensure that financial constraints do not hinder deserving students from pursuing their educational aspirations.

To benefit from these government policies and schemes, it's important to understand their eligibility criteria and application processes. Familiarise yourself with the specific requirements for each scheme, such as academic performance, family income limits, and any supporting documents that need to be submitted. This knowledge will enable you to determine your eligibility and apply for the schemes that align with your circumstances and educational goals.

When applying for government scholarships and schemes, ensure that you carefully follow the instructions and meet the application deadlines. Thoroughly review the guidelines provided by the respective authorities and provide accurate and complete information in your application. Take note of any required supporting documents, such as income certificates, educational transcripts, or other relevant proofs, and gather them in advance to streamline the application process.

Government policies and schemes play a significant role in making education more accessible and affordable for students. By taking advantage of these initiatives, you can alleviate the financial burden associated with pursuing higher education and create opportunities for a brighter future.

It's important fant to note that government policies and schemes are subject to change, and it's advisable to stay updated on any updates or modifications. Regularly visit the official websites of the government departments or scholarship portals to stay informed about new schemes, application deadlines, and any changes in eligibility criteria.

CHAPTER 19

ENTREPRENEURSHIP AND START-UP CULTURE

The rise of entrepreneurship in India has been remarkable in recent years. The country has witnessed a significant shift towards a vibrant start-up culture, with young entrepreneurs emerging as key contributors to the economy. These entrepreneurs have demonstrated their ability to innovate, disrupt traditional industries, and create successful businesses.

One of the driving factors behind the rise of entrepreneurship in India is the availability of resources and support for aspiring entrepreneurs. The government has implemented various initiatives and policies to promote entrepreneurship, including the "Start-up India" campaign and the establishment of incubation centres and funding programmes. These initiatives have created a conducive environment for young individuals to explore their entrepreneurial aspirations and transform their ideas into viable businesses.

The success stories of Indian start-ups, such as Flipkart, Ola, boat, Zomato and Lenskart have inspired a new generation of entrepreneurs. These stories showcase the potential for young individuals to make a significant impact and achieve success in the entrepreneurial landscape. The rise of entrepreneurship has also created a sense of optimism and a belief that anyone with a compelling idea and determination can create a successful business.

The increasing availability of venture capital funding and angel investments has also provided a boost to the start-up ecosystem in India.

Investors are now more willing to support early-stage ventures, providing the necessary capital for growth and expansion. This availability of funding has encouraged more individuals to take the entrepreneurial leap and pursue their business ideas.

The rise of entrepreneurship in India is not limited to specific sectors but spans a wide range of industries, including technology, e-commerce, healthcare, and finance. This diversification of entrepreneurial ventures reflects the dynamic nature of the Indian economy and the opportunities that exist in various sectors.

For young individuals, the rise of entrepreneurship in India presents an exciting opportunity. It offers a chance to be part of the entrepreneurial ecosystem, contribute to the country's economic growth, and create a positive impact. The success stories of young entrepreneurs who have overcome challenges achieved significant milestones, and transformed industries serve as inspiration and motivation for you to embark on your own entrepreneurial journey.

EXPLORING ENTREPRENEURSHIP: ITS SIGNIFICANCE FOR STUDENTS

Entrepreneurship is the process of identifying opportunities, taking risks, and creating innovative solutions to address societal needs or fulfil market demands. It involves starting, managing, and growing a business venture with the aim of creating value, making an impact, and generating profits. Entrepreneurship is not limited to starting new businesses but also encompasses the ability to bring about positive change within existing organisations and industries.

Today, entrepreneurship has become increasingly relevant to the youth. Here are some reasons why:

a. **Independence and Self-Determination:** Entrepreneurship offers the opportunity for individuals to be their own bosses and have control over their destinies. Many young people are drawn to the idea of creating their own path, pursuing their passions, and charting their own course rather than conforming to traditional career paths.

b. **Innovation and Creativity:** Entrepreneurship encourages and rewards innovation and creativity. It provides a platform for young individuals to think outside the box, challenge the status quo, and develop ground-breaking ideas and solutions. In an era of rapid technological advancements and changing market dynamics, entrepreneurial thinking is crucial for staying relevant and competitive.

c. **Job Creation:** With the rise of automation and the changing nature of work, traditional employment opportunities may become scarce. Entrepreneurship offers an avenue for young people to create their own jobs and become job creators rather than job seekers. By starting their own ventures, they not only generate employment for themselves but also create job opportunities for others.

d. **Impact and Purpose:** Many young individuals are driven by a desire to make a positive impact on society. Entrepreneurship provides a platform to address social and environmental challenges, create sustainable solutions, and contribute to the greater good. It allows young entrepreneurs to align their business goals with their values and create businesses that have a positive impact on people's lives.

e. **Learning and Personal Growth:** Entrepreneurship is a continuous learning journey. It requires individuals to be adaptable, resilient, and open to new experiences. Young entrepreneurs have the opportunity to acquire a diverse set of skills, gain practical knowledge, and develop their personal and professional capabilities. The challenges and obstacles they face along the way provide valuable learning experiences that contribute to their growth and development.

f. **Global Opportunities:** In today's interconnected world, entrepreneurship offers global opportunities. With the advent of technology and the ease of access to markets and resources, young entrepreneurs can start businesses with a global outlook from the start. They can leverage digital platforms to reach customers worldwide, collaborate with international partners, and tap into global networks and markets.

g. **Economic Growth and Development:** Entrepreneurship plays a crucial role in driving economic growth and development. Start-ups and small businesses contribute to job creation, innovation, and wealth generation. By encouraging and supporting young entrepreneurs, governments and societies can foster economic prosperity and build a thriving entrepreneurial ecosystem.

RESOURCES FOR STUDENT ENTREPRENEURS

As a student entrepreneur, you have access to valuable resources that can help you on your entrepreneurial journey. These resources provide mentorship, business development workshops, funding opportunities, and networking platforms to nurture your entrepreneurial spirit. Let us understand each one of them:

a. **Entrepreneurship Cells:** Many educational institutions have established entrepreneurship cells that serve as platforms for fostering an entrepreneurial culture on campus. For example, the Entrepreneurship Development Cell at the Indian Institute of Technology (IIT) Delhi organises events like E-Summit, which brings together budding entrepreneurs, investors, and industry experts. The cell also provides mentorship and networking opportunities through its start-up incubator.

b. **Incubation Centres:** Incubation centres provide comprehensive support to start-ups and early-stage ventures. The Start-up Incubation and Innovation Centre (SIIC) at IIT Kanpur is one such example. SIIC offers physical infrastructure, mentorship, and access to a network of experts. They have supported successful start-ups like Aerobotics7, which develops AI-based drones for precision agriculture, and Outgrow, a marketing software company.

c. **Entrepreneurship Development Programmes:** Institutions like the Indian School of Business (ISB) offer entrepreneurship development programmes. The Wadhwani Centre for Entrepreneurship Development at ISB conducts programmes like the Goldman Sachs 10,000 Women Entrepreneurs Program, providing women entrepreneurs with training, mentoring, and access to networks. These programmes equip students with the skills and knowledge needed to start and scale their ventures.

d. **Mentors and Experts:** Many institutions have mentorship programmes that connect student entrepreneurs with experienced mentors. The Student Entrepreneurship Programme at the Indian Institute of Management (IIM) Bangalore pairs students with industry mentors who provide guidance and support. This mentorship programme has helped student ventures like Reverie Language Technologies, a language localisation company, achieve significant growth.

e. **Funding Opportunities:** Various funding opportunities are available for student entrepreneurs. The National Science and Technology Entrepreneurship Development Board (NSTEDB) provides financial support through the Technology Business Incubator (TBI) scheme. Start-ups like AgNext, a precision agriculture technology company, have received funding from NSTEDB to develop their innovative solutions.

f. **Networking Platforms:** Networking platforms play a crucial role in connecting student entrepreneurs with industry experts and potential collaborators. TiE (The Indus Entrepreneurs) is a global network that hosts events and conferences, allowing student entrepreneurs to network with successful entrepreneurs and gain industry insights. TiE Delhi-NCR, for example, organises events like TiECon, bringing together entrepreneurs, investors, and industry leaders.

g. **Entrepreneurship Competitions and Challenges:** Participating in entrepreneurship competitions can provide valuable exposure and recognition. The Smart India Hackathon, organised by the Ministry of Education, invites students to solve real-world problems through innovation and technology. Winners receive cash prizes, mentorship, and support to further develop their solutions.

h. **Support Networks and Communities:** Engaging with support networks and communities can provide invaluable support and connections. The Entrepreneurship Development Institute of India (EDII) facilitates networking through its alumni network, where successful entrepreneurs share their experiences and mentor aspiring entrepreneurs. This community fosters collaboration and helps students access a wide range of resources.

These are just a few examples of the resources available for student entrepreneurs in India. It's essential to research and explore opportunities specific to your educational institution, local entrepreneurial ecosystem, and industry focus. By leveraging these resources, you can enhance your entrepreneurial journey and increase your chances of success.

Embracing entrepreneurship and the start-up culture can be an exciting and rewarding path for students like you.

FREQUENTLY ASKED QUESTIONS

Q. Do I have what it takes to be an entrepreneur?

A. Becoming an entrepreneur is not limited to a specific set of characteristics or traits. While certain qualities like creativity, resilience, and a willingness to take risks can be advantageous, entrepreneurship is a journey of continuous learning and growth. It's important to have a passion for your idea, a strong work ethic, and a willingness to adapt and learn from failures. With dedication, perseverance, and a growth mindset, anyone can develop the skills and mindset necessary to become a successful entrepreneur.

Q.   Do I need an MBA degree to pursue entrepreneurship?

A.   No, an MBA degree is not a strict requirement to become an entrepreneur. While an MBA can provide valuable knowledge and skills in areas such as business strategy, finance, marketing, and management, it is not the only path to entrepreneurial success. Many successful entrepreneurs have built their businesses without holding an MBA degree. The key to entrepreneurship is a combination of passion, determination, creativity, problem-solving abilities, and a willingness to continuously learn and adapt. While an MBA can provide a solid foundation, there are numerous other ways to gain the necessary skills and knowledge, such as real-world experience, networking, mentorship, and self-study. Ultimately, it depends on the individual's unique circumstances and the specific industry or sector they wish to enter.

Q.   How can I navigate the situation when my family doesn't support my pursuit of passion?

A.   It can be challenging when your family does not support your entrepreneurial aspirations. However, it's important to have open and honest conversations with your family to understand their concerns and share your vision and passion. Try to address their worries by presenting a well-researched business plan, showcasing the potential benefits, and explaining your commitment to success. You can also seek support from mentors, advisers, or entrepreneurship networks who can provide guidance and help you navigate this situation.

Q.   What if I fail in my venture?

A.   Failure is a part of the entrepreneurial journey, and many successful entrepreneurs have experienced setbacks along the way. It's important to remember that failure is an opportunity for learning and growth.

Analyse the reasons for the failure, adapt your approach, and use the experience to make more informed decisions in the future. Surround yourself with a supportive network of mentors and peers who can provide guidance and encouragement. Remember, failure is not the end, but rather a stepping stone towards future success.

Q. How will I get the money to fund my business?

A. Securing funding for your business can be a challenge, but there are several options available. Start by assessing your financial needs and creating a comprehensive business plan. You can explore traditional funding sources such as bank loans, government schemes, or venture capital firms. Additionally, consider alternative funding methods like crowdfunding, angel investors, or grants specifically designed for start-ups. Networking and building relationships with potential investors or attending entrepreneurship events can also help you connect with funding opportunities.

Q. When is the ideal time to start a business, right after completing studies or after gaining work experience?

A. The right time to start a business varies for each individual and depends on factors such as your readiness, market conditions, and personal circumstances. Some entrepreneurs choose to start their ventures immediately after studies to capitalise on their fresh knowledge and enthusiasm, while others prefer gaining experience in the industry to develop skills and build networks before starting a business.

Q. What are the job prospects if I choose to work later?

A. Regarding job prospects, having entrepreneurial experience can be valuable even if you decide to work later. Many employers value the skills and mindset gained through entrepreneurship, such as initiative, problem-solving, and adaptability. It's important to highlight your entrepreneurial experience on your resume and during interviews to showcase your unique skills and perspective.

Q. **Is support for starting a business limited to large institutions or is it also available in small cities?**

A. Support for entrepreneurs is not limited to large institutions or cities. While larger institutions may have more established entrepreneurship programmes and resources, there are initiatives and organisations supporting entrepreneurship in smaller cities as well. Local business incubators, entrepreneurship cells, and industry associations can provide valuable support, mentorship, and networking opportunities. Additionally, online platforms and communities offer resources and connections for entrepreneurs regardless of their location.

Q. **I want to start my business but I don't have the right skills & knowledge.**

A. If you want to start a business but feel like you lack the required skills and knowledge, don't worry! Here are some steps you can take to acquire the necessary skills and knowledge:

    a. **Identify the skills and knowledge you need:** Start by determining the specific skills and knowledge that are essential for your business idea. Consider the industry you want to enter, the nature of your business, and the roles you'll be taking on. This will help you prioritise your learning efforts.

    b. **Invest in self-education:** There are numerous resources available to help you acquire skills and knowledge independently. You can start by reading books, articles, and online resources related to your industry. Online learning platforms such as Coursera, Udemy, and LinkedIn Learning offer courses on a wide range of topics, including entrepreneurship, marketing, finance, and more.

    c. **Seek formal education or training:** If you feel that you need a more structured approach, consider pursuing formal education or training programmes. Look for courses, workshops, or certifications offered by reputable institutions or organisations.

Business schools, community colleges, and vocational institutes often provide relevant programmes tailored for aspiring entrepreneurs.

d. **Find a mentor or adviser:** Connecting with experienced entrepreneurs or industry professionals can provide valuable guidance and mentorship. Seek out individuals who have expertise in your desired field and are willing to share their knowledge and insights. They can offer practical advice, help you navigate challenges, and provide valuable networking opportunities.

e. **Join entrepreneurship networks and communities:** Engaging with like-minded individuals can help you expand your knowledge and skills. Join local entrepreneurship networks, attend industry events, and participate in online communities or forums. These platforms provide opportunities for learning, networking, and collaboration with fellow entrepreneurs.

f. **Gain practical experience through internships or apprenticeships:** Consider seeking internships or apprenticeships with established entrepreneurs or businesses in your industry. This hands-on experience will give you valuable insights, allow you to learn from experienced professionals, and help you develop the skills necessary to run your own business.

Remember, entrepreneurship is a personal journey, and there is no one-size-fits-all approach. It's important to trust your instincts, seek guidance from experienced mentors, and continuously learn and adapt as you pursue your entrepreneurial aspirations.

CHAPTER 20

NURTURING MEANINGFUL CONNECTIONS

In this journey of success, the management of relationships holds immense importance, serving as a vital component that shapes both academic and personal growth. This chapter aims to provide practical guidance and insights into the importance of building positive and meaningful relationships with classmates, professors, mentors, and support staff. We will explore effective communication strategies, conflict resolution techniques, and the significance of leveraging relationships for personal and academic development.

BUILDING POSITIVE AND MEANINGFUL RELATIONSHIPS

To foster a welcoming and inclusive environment, actively engage with your classmates by participating in discussions, collaborating on group projects, and getting involved in extracurricular activities. Take the initiative to find common interests, support one another, and build connections that contribute to a supportive academic community. By creating a sense of belonging and camaraderie, you'll not only enhance your own experience but also create a positive environment for others.

In addition to cultivating relationships with your peers, it's crucial to initiate conversations with professors, mentors, and support staff.

These individuals are there to guide and support you throughout your academic journey. Take advantage of opportunities like office hours to connect with them, seek their advice, and share your academic goals and challenges. By developing a rapport with them, you can benefit from their expertise, receive valuable insights, and build relationships based on mutual respect and trust.

Remember, relationships are a two-way street. Be attentive and considerate when engaging with others, actively listen to their perspectives, and show genuine interest in their experiences. Building strong relationships takes time and effort, but the rewards are invaluable. By investing in meaningful connections, you create a support system that can positively impact your academic and personal growth.

Here are some practical tips to help you in managing relationships effectively:

1. Be proactive in initiating conversations and building connections.

2. Actively listen to others and show genuine interest in their thoughts and experiences.

3. Create opportunities to collaborate and work together on projects.

4. Respect and appreciate diversity, fostering an inclusive environment.

5. Attend office hours and seek guidance from professors and mentors.

6. Participate in extracurricular activities to meet new people and expand your network.

7. Show appreciation and gratitude for the support you receive from others.

8. Be open to constructive feedback and use it as an opportunity for growth.

9. Express your thoughts and concerns clearly and respectfully.

10. Be a supportive and reliable peer, offering help and assistance when needed.

By implementing these tips, you can cultivate meaningful relationships that contribute to your overall success in higher education. Remember, the connections you build during your academic journey can have a lasting impact on your personal and professional life.

EFFECTIVE COMMUNICATION

Effective communication is a vital skill for success in higher education and beyond. It allows you to express your thoughts, ideas, and concerns clearly and respectfully, while also fostering understanding and collaboration with others. Here are some practical tips to develop strong communication skills:

1. **Active Listening:** Actively listen to others when they are speaking. Give them your full attention, maintain eye contact, and avoid interrupting. Ask questions for clarification and show genuine interest in what they have to say.

2. **Clarity and Conciseness:** Express your thoughts and ideas in a clear and concise manner. Organise your ideas before communicating and use appropriate language for your audience. Avoid using jargon or complex terminology that may confuse others.

3. **Choose the Right Medium:** Consider the most appropriate communication channel for your message. For formal or important matters, face-to-face interactions or emails may be more suitable. For quick queries or informal discussions, online platforms or instant messaging can be more efficient.

4. **Professionalism:** Maintain professionalism in your communication. Use a polite and respectful tone, regardless of the situation. Pay attention to grammar, spelling,

and punctuation to ensure your messages are clear and professional.

5. **Timeliness:** Respond to messages and emails promptly. Avoid unnecessary delays in your communication, as it shows respect for others' time and demonstrates your commitment to effective communication.

6. **Non-Verbal Communication:** Be aware of your non-verbal cues, such as body language, facial expressions, and gestures. Maintain open and attentive body language to show your engagement and interest in the conversation.

7. **Cultural Sensitivity:** Be mindful of cultural differences in communication styles and norms. Respect and adapt to diverse communication preferences and practices to ensure effective cross-cultural communication.

8. **Practice and ask for Feedback:** Practice your communication skills regularly, both in academic and personal settings. Ask for feedback from trusted individuals, such as professors or mentors, to identify areas for improvement and continue refining your communication skills.

Remember, effective communication is a continuous learning process. By developing strong communication skills, you can enhance your interactions with classmates, professors, and support staff, fostering meaningful relationships and creating a positive academic environment.

CONFLICT RESOLUTION

Conflict resolution is an important skill that can help you navigate challenging situations and maintain positive relationships in your academic journey. Here are some practical tips for effectively resolving conflicts:

1. **Empathy and Understanding:** Try to understand the other person's point of view and put yourself in their shoes. Recognise that everyone has different experiences and perspectives that

may contribute to the conflict. Show empathy and validate their emotions to foster a sense of understanding.

2. **Find Common Ground:** Look for areas of agreement or shared interests to find common ground. Focus on common goals or objectives that can help in resolving the conflict and moving forward. This can create a basis for finding mutually beneficial solutions.

3. **Respectful Communication:** Maintain a respectful and constructive tone during conflict resolution conversations. Avoid blaming or criticising the other person and instead focus on expressing your concerns and needs. Use "I" statements to express your thoughts and feelings without placing blame on others.

4. **Problem-Solving Approach:** Approach conflicts with a problem-solving mindset. Collaboratively explore different solutions and brainstorm ideas that can address the underlying issues. Be open to compromise and be willing to find win-win solutions that benefit all parties involved.

5. **Seek Guidance:** If you are facing challenges in your relationships with professors or mentors, don't hesitate to approach them respectfully and express your concerns. Seek guidance or clarification from them to gain a better understanding of the situation and find a resolution. They can provide valuable insights and support in resolving conflicts.

6. **Mediation or Third-Party Involvement:** In some cases, it may be helpful to involve a neutral third-party, such as a mediator or adviser, to facilitate the conflict resolution process. They can provide an unbiased perspective and help facilitate productive communication between the parties involved.

Remember, conflicts are a natural part of human interaction, and how you handle them can have a significant impact on your relationships and overall academic experience.

MANAGING ROMANTIC RELATIONSHIPS

College life is a time of growth and exploration, which may include the experience of romantic relationships. While love affairs can be fulfilling, it's important to navigate them in a way that maintains a healthy balance with academic commitments. This section aims to provide practical tips and insights on managing love affairs without compromising on career goals, based on real-life experiences and data.

Research has shown that romantic relationships in college can have both positive and negative impacts on academic performance. On one hand, being in a supportive and loving relationship can provide emotional stability and motivation, which may contribute to better academic outcomes. On the other hand, when relationships become a source of distraction, conflict, or excessive time and energy investment, they can negatively affect focus, time management, and overall academic success.

Practical Tips for Managing Love Affairs without Compromising Career Goals:

- **Set Mutual Expectations:** Communicate openly and honestly with your partner about your career aspirations and the importance of academic success. Discuss mutual expectations regarding the time and effort you both will invest in your respective goals, ensuring that you share a common understanding and commitment to support each other's ambitions.

- **Plan Together:** Collaborate with your partner to create a shared schedule that allows dedicated time for both academic pursuits and quality time together. This includes setting aside specific study periods, as well as planned leisure activities or date nights, to maintain a healthy balance between work and personal life.

- **Self-Discipline:** Cultivate self-discipline and time management skills to stay focused on your academic responsibilities. Avoid procrastination, establish realistic study goals, and create a study environment that minimises distractions. By maintaining a disciplined approach, you can allocate sufficient time for your relationship while ensuring your academic progress remains on track.

⅄ **Supportive Partnerships:** Surround yourself with a partner who understands and supports your career goals. Choose someone who respects your dedication to your studies and encourages your pursuit of academic success. A supportive partner can provide emotional support, help manage stress, and celebrate your achievements, creating a healthy and motivating relationship dynamic.

⅄ **Reflect on Personal Growth:** Regularly assess your personal growth and academic progress. Reflect on how your relationship aligns with your long-term goals and evaluate whether it is positively contributing to your overall well-being and success. Be willing to make adjustments and have open discussions with your partner if needed.

Love affairs can be a wonderful part of the college experience, but it's important to manage them in a way that doesn't compromise your career goals and overall success. Striking a healthy balance between personal relationships and career aspirations will contribute to your overall fulfilment and success in both areas of your life.

Mental Health and Well-being

Maintaining good mental health is crucial for your overall well-being and academic success. Here are some practical tips to prioritise your mental health and well-being during your college journey:

1. **Establish a Work-Life Balance:** Strive for a healthy balance between your academic commitments and personal life. Set realistic expectations for yourself and avoid overloading your schedule. Schedule regular breaks, engage in hobbies or activities you enjoy, and spend time with friends and family. Finding a balance between work and relaxation will help reduce stress and improve your overall well-being.

2. **Ask for help:** If you find yourself facing challenges or feeling overwhelmed, don't hesitate to seek support. Most colleges and universities offer counselling services where you can talk to a professional about your concerns. Additionally, reach out to trusted friends, family members, or mentors who can provide a listening ear and offer guidance. Remember, seeking support is a sign of strength, not weakness.

3. **Foster a Supportive Community:** Surround yourself with a supportive network of friends and peers who uplift and encourage you. Build relationships based on empathy, understanding, and mutual support. Engage in positive social interactions and participate in campus activities or clubs that align with your interests. Being part of a supportive community can provide a sense of belonging and contribute to your overall well-being.

4. **Manage Stress:** Develop healthy coping mechanisms to manage stress effectively. This may include deep breathing exercises, practising mindfulness or meditation, journalling, or engaging in creative outlets such as art or music. Experiment with different techniques and identify what works best for you to reduce stress and promote relaxation.

5. **Be Mindful of Your Mental Health:** Pay attention to your mental and emotional well-being. Recognise signs of distress, such as changes in mood, sleep patterns, or concentration levels. If you notice persistent feelings of anxiety, sadness, or difficulty coping, seek professional help. Your college's counselling services or mental health resources can provide valuable guidance and support.

Remember, taking care of your mental health is not only important for your well-being but also for your academic success. By taking the above steps, you can enhance your overall well-being and create a positive college experience.

Case Study Inspired by a Real-life Incident:

Reena's (name hidden) Journey to Recovery and Rediscovery

Reena, a talented and dedicated student pursuing B.Tech at a prestigious university in North India, had always been an exceptional performer academically and actively participated in various extracurricular activities. She was well-respected by her peers and admired by her professors for her determination and achievements.

During her third year of studies, Reena entered into a serious relationship with a fellow student. Initially, the relationship seemed promising and brought happiness to her life. However, over time, conflicts and disagreements began to arise, leading to frequent arguments and emotional turmoil.

As the relationship deteriorated, Reena's focus on her studies started to diminish. She found it increasingly challenging to concentrate on her coursework, attend classes regularly, and complete assignments on time. Her grades, which were once exemplary, began to decline, affecting her overall academic performance.

The emotional distress caused by the failed relationship took a toll on Reena's mental well-being. She experienced a loss of motivation, self-doubt, and a lack of confidence in her abilities. Her once strong drive to succeed and pursue her career goals waned, and she felt lost and uncertain about her future.

Reena's decline in academic performance and lack of focus affected her chances of securing internships and participating in campus recruitment drives. She missed out on valuable opportunities to gain industry exposure, develop professional connections, and secure job offers from reputed companies.

Recovery and Rediscovery:

Realising the detrimental impact the failed relationship was having on her life, Reena made a brave decision to prioritise her well-being and academic success. She sought support from a career coach to help her navigate through the challenging phase.

She worked closely with her coach to develop a study schedule, set achievable goals, and implement effective time management strategies. Through consistent effort and determination, she gradually regained her confidence and began to excel academically once again.

During the process, Reena realised the importance of rediscovering her passions and interests outside of her relationship. She re-engaged with extracurricular activities, joining clubs and participating in events that aligned with her interests. This helped her regain a sense of purpose, build new friendships, and find joy beyond her academic pursuits.

Reena's case highlights the challenges faced by students when navigating personal relationships while pursuing academic and career goals. The story serves as a reminder that setbacks should not define one's entire journey and that with the determination and support of good friends, it is possible to regain focus, rebuild confidence, and pursue a successful career.

CHAPTER 21

DECODING THE COOL CULTURE: IMPACT ON YOUTH AND CAREERS

In recent years, there has been a noticeable shift in the culture within Indian colleges and universities, with the emergence of what is commonly referred to as the "cool culture". This cultural transformation has had a significant impact on the youth, influencing their behaviours, attitudes, and career choices. The culture has become synonymous with the traits of Gen Z, representing a generation that values non-conformity, instant gratification, and adventurous pursuits.

While acknowledging the allure of this culture, the focus must shift towards empowering the youth to make informed choices rather than being pulled under the pressure of a lack of awareness. This chapter explores the significance of drawing a line in the cool culture and sensitising the youth about the importance of making conscious decisions that align with their values and aspirations.

As we explore this cool culture, we must also acknowledge the concerning influence of smoking, drinking and drugs on the youth. These elements have become prevalent in the college lifestyle and can significantly impact the physical and mental well-being of young individuals.

THE COOL CULTURE

THE PERCEPTION OF COOLNESS

The cool culture as I mentioned above is characterised by a focus on non-conformity, seeking instant gratification, and embracing an image of being carefree and adventurous. It often includes elements such as highly-casual dressing, indulgence in social media, weekend partying, hyper-emphasis on appearance, popularity and substance use. Students might believe that indulging in such behaviours makes them more socially accepted or enhances their image of being adventurous and carefree.

PEER PRESSURE AND FOMO

Social media platforms play a significant role in promoting and shaping this cool culture. Movies, web series, influencers, and celebrities often portray a glamourised version of college life, which influences young minds and sets unrealistic expectations. The desire to fit into the cool culture can lead to peer pressure, where students feel compelled to engage in such acts including substance abuse to avoid exclusion or ridicule. Fear of missing out (FOMO) on social experiences can also drive young individuals to participate in activities they may not be comfortable with.

IMPACT ON PERSONAL DEVELOPMENT

- **Delayed Maturity**

  The pursuit of an image associated with being cool can sometimes lead to delayed emotional and social maturity. Young adults may prioritise seeking instant pleasure and popularity over long-term personal growth and responsible decision-making.

- **Physical Health Risks**

  The use of smoking and excessive drinking poses severe health risks. Students may experience short-term effects like impaired cognitive function and concentration, as well as long-term health issues that can hinder their overall well-being and performance.

⅄ **Mental Health Consequences**

Substance abuse can contribute to mental health problems, including anxiety, depression, and addiction. This not only affects a student's academic performance but also hampers personal growth and development.

⅄ **Deterioration of Academic Performance**

Regular indulgence can lead to a decline in academic performance. Students may struggle to focus on their studies, meet deadlines, or attend classes consistently, impacting their grades and future career opportunities.

IMPACT ON CAREER PROSPECTS

⅄ **Employability and Professional Image:**

The cool culture may distract students from developing essential employability skills, such as time management, communication, critical thinking, and professionalism. These skills are vital for career success but might be overlooked in favour of more immediate gratifications. Frequent indulgence can damage a student's professional image and employability.

⅄ **Networking and Career Relationships:**

Building strong professional networks and maintaining positive relationships with mentors and professors are critical for career advancement. However nonchalance and casual attitudes might hinder the development of these crucial connections. A reputation associated with such behaviour may deter potential mentors, employers, or colleagues from investing in a student's career advancement.

⅄ **Missed Opportunities:**

The cool culture's focus on immediate gratification can lead students to prioritise short-term experiences over long-term career goals. This may result in missed opportunities for internships, career fairs, and skill development programmes that can shape their professional trajectory.

ENCOURAGING RESPONSIBLE CHOICES FOR A SUCCESSFUL FUTURE

⋏ Raising Awareness

Educational institutions and student bodies should work together to raise awareness about the harmful effects of smoking & drinking. Implementing educational programmes and workshops can empower students to make informed and responsible choices.

⋏ Support Systems and Counselling

Colleges and universities should provide accessible counselling services and support systems for students struggling with such issues. Encouraging an open dialogue about mental health and addiction can help those in need seek assistance.

⋏ Fostering a Positive Environment

Promote a positive and inclusive college environment that celebrates diversity and personal growth. Encourage students to find alternative avenues for socialising and bonding that do not revolve around excessive social media use or drinking & smoking.

The impact of drugs, smoking, and drinking goes beyond health risks and can have lasting effects on personal development and career prospects.

STAYING TRUE TO YOURSELF: HOW TO SAY NO

Saying no to indulging in any act that your conscience doesn't allow can be challenging, but it's essential to uphold your values and maintain personal integrity. Here are some tips on how to do it:

i. **Stay True to Your Values:** Remind yourself of your core beliefs and values. Knowing what you stand for will make it easier to say no when faced with situations that contradict your principles.

ii. **Be Confident and Assertive:** Speak firmly and assertively when declining to participate in something that goes against your conscience. Use clear language to express your decision without feeling apologetic.

iii. **Explain Your Reasons (Optional):** If you feel comfortable, you can briefly explain why you're saying no. Keep it simple and avoid getting defensive. Most people will respect your decision when they understand your perspective.

iv. **Set Boundaries:** Establish personal boundaries and communicate them to others. Let them know what you are comfortable with and what crosses the line for you.

v. **Don't Succumb to Peer Pressure:** Stand your ground even if others are trying to persuade you to do something you don't want to do. Remember that it's okay to be different and make choices that align with your conscience.

vi. **Offer Alternatives:** If possible, suggest alternative activities or solutions that align with your values. This shows that you are still willing to engage without compromising your beliefs.

vii. **Surround Yourself with Supportive People:** Surround yourself with friends and acquaintances who respect your choices and encourage you to stay true to yourself. Positive influences can make it easier to resist negative peer pressure.

viii. **Practice Saying No:** Role-play or practice saying no in front of a mirror. This can boost your confidence and make it easier to respond when the situation arises.

ix. **Don't Feel Guilty:** It's natural to feel a bit guilty for saying no, especially if it involves disappointing others. However, remember that prioritising your conscience is essential for your well-being and personal growth.

x. **Learn from the Experience:** Every time you say no to something that doesn't align with your conscience, you reinforce your values and grow stronger in your convictions. Reflect on these experiences and use them as opportunities for self-improvement.

Remember, SAYING NO is not a sign of weakness; it's a demonstration of self-respect and inner strength. Trust yourself and be proud of your ability to make choices that align with your conscience and lead you towards a more authentic and fulfilling life.

SPIRITUALITY & STUDENT SUCCESS

I've personally come to believe that spirituality holds significant importance, particularly during the crucial formative years of higher education. To me, spirituality goes beyond adhering to any specific religious doctrine; it's about deepening our self-awareness and our connection to the world around us. True success, I believe, is unattainable until we recognise the broader purpose of our existence. It's during this phase that the search for meaning commences, laying the firm groundwork for our adult lives.

WHAT DOES "SPIRITUALITY" ACTUALLY MEAN FOR STUDENTS?

Let's kick things off by demystifying spirituality, it's not about rituals or religious labels; it's about you and your quest for meaning and inner peace. Think of it as your personal GPS for navigating the turbulent waters of higher education. It's the light that guides you through both your academic and life journeys.

"Spirituality" is a term that can mean different things to different people, including students. For students, spirituality often represents a personal and inner journey to explore the deeper aspects of life beyond the material and physical world. It involves seeking a sense of purpose, meaning, and connection to something greater than oneself.

Here are a few key aspects of what spirituality might mean for students:

a. **Self-Discovery:** Spirituality can be a path to self-discovery, helping students understand themselves on a profound level. It involves asking questions about one's beliefs, values, and the purpose of their life.

b. **Inner Peace:** Many students turn to spirituality as a way to find inner peace and emotional balance, especially in the midst of the challenges and stresses of higher education.

c. **Connection:** Spirituality often involves a sense of connection, whether it's with the universe, nature, other people, or a higher power. It can provide a feeling of belonging and interconnectedness.

d. **Meaning and Purpose**: Students may explore spirituality to seek a deeper meaning and purpose in their lives. It can help them understand why they are pursuing their academic and personal goals.

e. **Values and Ethics:** Spirituality can influence students' values and ethical principles. It can encourage them to live more compassionately, ethically, and in harmony with their beliefs.

f. **Growth and Transformation:** Spirituality can be a catalyst for personal growth and transformation, inspiring students to evolve as individuals and contribute positively to society.

Remember that spirituality is highly individualised, and its meaning can vary greatly from person to person. Some students may find it through religious practices, while others may explore it through meditation, nature, or philosophical inquiries. Ultimately, spirituality is about the journey of self-discovery and personal growth, which can be a valuable and enriching aspect of the student experience.

THE NUTS AND BOLTS OF SPIRITUAL PRACTICE

You might wonder, "How do I actually practice spirituality?" Well, there's no one-size-fits-all answer. It's a customisable journey. Here are some practical tips to get you started:

a. **Mindfulness Matters:** Take a moment to pause, take a deep breath, and be fully present in the here and now. Mindfulness techniques, like meditation or even mindful walks, help you connect with your inner self, especially when things get busy with college work.

b. **Explore Widely:** Don't limit yourself. Learn from many different sources, talk to people with various beliefs, and try to understand spirituality from different angles. It's like expanding your knowledge about the world of spirituality.

c. **Keep a Spiritual Diary:** Write down your thoughts and feelings regularly. This diary helps you see how you're growing spiritually over time. It's like keeping track of your personal journey.

d. **Gratitude Rituals:** Every day, take a moment to think about the good things in your life and say "thank you" for them. It's a simple but powerful way to find inner happiness.

e. **Serve Others:** Set aside some time to help others. Doing kind things for people is a way of showing your spirituality in action.

Remember, there's no one right way to practice spirituality. It's all about what works best for you, and these tips are just a starting point to help you explore and find your own path.

THE COMPASSION CONNECTION

Let's take a closer look at the idea of compassion and why it's not just a lofty idea but a practical and essential tool for your success in higher education.

Compassion, at its core, is about understanding and caring for others and yourself. It's not something abstract; it's a real-life skill that can make your college experience smoother and more fulfilling.

a. **Start with Self-Compassion:** Imagine you're juggling deadlines, exams, and the challenges of college life. It can get overwhelming. This is where self-compassion comes in. Instead of being overly critical of yourself, treat yourself kindly. Acknowledge that you're human, and it's okay to make mistakes or have tough days. Self-compassion is like a comforting hand on your shoulder during those stressful times, reminding you to be gentle with yourself.

b. **Extend Compassion Outward:** As you progress through your academic journey, you'll encounter fellow students facing their unique challenges. Some might be struggling with coursework, others with personal issues. This is where you have the opportunity to put compassion into practice. It's not just a concept; it's a real, tangible action.

Now Imagine a classmate who's struggling to keep up. Instead of judging or ignoring their difficulties, you can lend a listening ear or offer help when appropriate. Compassion is like a bridge that connects you with others, creating a supportive and understanding academic environment.

When you practice compassion towards yourself and others, you not only make your own campus journey manageable but also contribute to a more compassionate and empathetic community.

THE VALUE OF VALUES

Values and spirituality share common ground in their quest for meaning, ethical guidance, and personal growth. While value systems provide a practical framework for living ethically, spirituality often provides the philosophical and contemplative depth that enriches our understanding of why certain values are important. Together, they can create a harmonious and purposeful way of living that benefits not only the individual but also the broader community and society.

Values are like the guiding stars that help you navigate the complex terrain of education, careers and life beyond. A value system consists of principles and beliefs that dictate our actions, decisions, and interactions with others. Developing a strong value system is not just about being morally upright; it's about consciously choosing the kind of person you want to become and the impact you wish to have on the world.

Higher education serves as the crucible where values are refined and solidified. It's a time when students are exposed to diverse ideas, cultures, and perspectives. This exposure can either reinforce existing values or challenge them, leading to personal growth and development.

In the pursuit of knowledge, students have the opportunity to examine their beliefs critically, consider different viewpoints, and refine their value system. This process is essential because it not only equips them with academic prowess but also shapes their character and prepares them for the challenges of the professional world.

Building a Solid Foundation for Careers

A strong value system is a valuable asset in the world of work. Here's how it can pave the way for successful careers:

a. **Integrity:** Upholding honesty and moral principles in your professional life builds trust with colleagues and employers. It's the foundation of a reputable and sustainable career.

b. **Work Ethic:** Values like dedication, perseverance, and responsibility drive a strong work ethic. These qualities are highly prized by employers and can lead to career advancement.

c. **Teamwork:** Values that emphasise collaboration and respect for others' opinions are crucial in a workplace that often requires teamwork. A strong value system helps foster effective working relationships.

d. **Leadership:** Values like empathy, fairness, and a commitment to social responsibility are qualities often found in effective leaders. They inspire trust and confidence in others, facilitating career progression.

A Society Less Judgemental and More Supportive

Beyond personal success, a robust value system contributes to the broader society. It helps create a culture that is less judgemental and more supportive. When individuals hold values like tolerance, empathy, and inclusivity, they contribute to a society where differences are celebrated rather than stigmatised.

a. **Tolerance:** A strong value system that promotes tolerance encourages individuals to accept and respect diverse perspectives, beliefs, and backgrounds. This reduces prejudice and fosters a more inclusive society.

b. **Empathy:** Values rooted in empathy enable individuals to understand and share the feelings of others. Empathy promotes kindness, compassion, and a willingness to support those in need.

c. **Supportive Communities:** When people uphold values of community, they create environments where individuals are more willing to help one another, leading to stronger, more connected societies.

d. **Social Responsibility:** A value system that includes a commitment to social responsibility motivates individuals to contribute to the welfare of their communities and address societal issues.

Ultimately, a strong value system is an invaluable asset that goes hand in hand with academic achievement. It prepares students not only for successful careers but also for a more harmonious and supportive society. As students in higher education, remember that the values you embrace today have the potential to shape the world you'll lead tomorrow.

The ABCs of Student Success: A Simple Framework

A – Academic Excellence:

Strive for academic excellence by staying organised, managing your time effectively, attending classes regularly, and actively engaging with your coursework. Seek help when needed, and never stop learning.

B – Build Relationships:

Nurture meaningful relationships with professors, classmates, and mentors. Collaboration and networking are keys to success. Don't hesitate to ask questions and seek guidance; people are there to support you.

C – Cultivate Balance:

Maintain a healthy work-life balance. Take care of your physical and mental well-being through regular exercise, proper nutrition, and self-care. Balance academics with extracurricular activities and downtime.

D – Define Goals:

Set clear, achievable goals for both the short-term and long-term. Having a roadmap will keep you motivated and focused. Periodically review and adjust your goals as needed.

E – Embrace Challenges:

Don't shy away from challenges; see them as opportunities for growth. Resilience is key. Learn from failures, adapt, and keep moving forward.

F – Foster Curiosity:

Cultivate your curiosity and love for learning. Be open to exploring new subjects, ideas, and experiences. A curious mind is a powerful tool for personal and professional development.

G – Give Back:

Give back to your community and society. Volunteer, engage in service projects, and use your skills and knowledge to make a positive impact on the world.

H – Harness Resources:

Utilise the resources available to you, including libraries, academic support services, and career centres. Seek scholarships, internships, and opportunities that align with your goals.

I – Integrity Matters:

Maintain honesty and integrity in all your endeavours. Uphold ethical principles, and build a reputation as a trustworthy and principled individual.

J – Journey of Self-Discovery:

Embrace the journey of self-discovery. Understand your strengths, weaknesses, passions, and values. Self-awareness is the foundation for personal and professional growth.

K – Keep Perspective:

Maintain a balanced perspective on success. It's not just about grades or achievements but about personal growth, resilience, and making a positive impact on the world.

L – Lifelong Learning:

Commit to lifelong learning. Education doesn't end with graduation. Continuously seek opportunities to expand your knowledge and skills throughout your life.

M – Manage Stress:

Develop effective stress management strategies, such as mindfulness, relaxation techniques, and time management. Stress is a part of life; how you handle it matters.

N – Network Wisely:

Build a diverse and supportive network of contacts. Your network can open doors, provide valuable insights, and offer guidance as you navigate your career path.

O – Overcome Obstacles:

Expect obstacles and setbacks, but don't let them define you. Use them as stepping stones to move forward and grow stronger.

P – Persevere:

Perseverance is key to success. Stay committed to your goals, even when faced with challenges. Remember that setbacks are temporary, but your determination is enduring.

Q – Question and Reflect:

Continually question assumptions, challenge your beliefs, and reflect on your experiences. Critical thinking and self-reflection are essential for personal development.

R – Resilience Matters:

Cultivate resilience by developing a growth mindset. Embrace setbacks as opportunities to learn and adapt. Resilience is your armour against adversity.

S – Seek Mentorship:

Find mentors who can guide and inspire you. Seek advice from those who have walked a similar path and learn from their experiences.

T – Take Initiative:

Don't wait for opportunities to come to you; take initiative and create them. Be proactive in pursuing your goals and ambitions.

U – Unwavering Commitment:

Stay committed to your values, principles, and ethical standards. Your integrity and commitment will define your character.

V – Visualise Success:

Mentally visualise your success and the path to achieving your goals. Visualisation can be a powerful motivator.

W – Work Ethic:

Cultivate a strong work ethic. Consistent effort and diligence are the building blocks of achievement.

X – X Factor

It's a reminder that you possess your own unique strengths and attributes that can contribute to your personal growth and success in the higher educational journey and beyond. Never compare yourself with anyone.

Y – Yearn for Knowledge:

Never lose your thirst for knowledge. Approach each day with a hunger to learn and grow.

Z – Zero Regrets:

Live with purpose and passion, so you can look back on your journey with zero regrets. Make the most of every opportunity and embrace life to the fullest.

Remember, success is not a destination; it's a lifelong journey. Use my ABCs framework as a guide, adapt it to your unique circumstances, and keep striving for personal and professional excellence. Your success story is waiting to be written.

Conclusion & Path Ahead

Congratulations, dear friends, for embarking on this transformative journey through *This Is How We Do It: Student Success in Higher Education and Beyond.* As you now stand at the cusp of your academic and professional pursuits, I hope this book has ignited a newfound passion and sense of purpose within you.

Throughout these pages, we have explored the essence of true success, transcending the limitations of conventional metrics. I trust that you now possess invaluable strategies to navigate the complexities of higher education and the job market. As you explore promising career opportunities, I hope you feel empowered to embrace your unique path to success.

As we conclude, I encourage you to foster meaningful relationships and mental health throughout your journey. With an entrepreneurial spirit, explore your potential as a visionary leader who can impact the world positively. Remember, the essence of *This Is How We Do It* is not just within these pages but within you. Let your passion, purpose, and unwavering determination be the guiding forces towards lasting success and fulfilment.

I invite you to stay connected through my website, www. thecorporatepolitics.com, where I stand ready to offer guidance and support as you continue your higher education journey and beyond.

With boundless possibilities ahead, let us do it together, creating an extraordinary future that knows no bounds.

This is not just the end; it is the beginning of your extraordinary story.

About the Author

Ajay Khanna is a dedicated people development professional with over two decades of leadership experience in the realms of professional training and higher education. His unwavering commitment to empowering students and professionals has left a profound impact on the lives of over 30,000 individuals.

With a distinguished background as the Director of Student Success at India's leading private universities, Ajay brings a wealth of practical experience and insights to the table. Today, he stands as a full-time social entrepreneur and the founder of "The Corporate Politics", a prominent professional training and coaching company.

Ajay's relentless pursuit of student success has led him to create multiple strategies to guide aspiring individuals in their journey of higher education and beyond. He offers free guidance and support to thousands of students and young professionals, helping them navigate their careers with confidence and clarity.

REFERENCES

1. https://www.nafsa.org/ie-magazine/2022/4/12/indias-higher-education-landscape

2. Global Workplace Analytics. (2021). Remote Work Statistics. Retrieved from https://globalworkplaceanalytics.com/remote-work-statistics

3. The Balance Careers. (2021). How to Use the STAR Interview Response Technique. Retrieved from https://www.thebalancecareers.com/what-is-the-star-interview-response-technique-2061629

4. Intuit. (2020). Dispatches from the New Economy: The On-Demand Workforce. Retrieved from https://www.intuit.com/content/dam/intuit/infographic/dispatches-from-the-new-economy-infographic.pdf

5. Front. Educ., 29 March 2022 Educational Psychology

6. Glassdoor. (2021). 50 Common Interview Questions and Answers. Retrieved from https://www.glassdoor.com/blog/common-interview-questions/

7. Glassdoor. (n.d.). How to Research a Company: A Complete Guide. Retrieved from https://www.glassdoor.com/research/how-to-research-a-company/

8. The Balance Careers. (2021). How to Practice for a Job Interview. Retrieved from https://www.thebalancecareers.com/how-to-practice-for-a-job-interview-2061336

9 7 9 8 8 9 0 6 7 7 0 6 8